8.9'78

# CAREERS
## A Guide for Parents and Counselors

# Careers

A Guide for Parents and Counselors

Darryl Laramore

Brigham Young University Press

**Library of Congress Cataloging in Publication Data**

Laramore, Darryl, 1928–
  Careers.

  1. Vocational guidance. I. Title.
HF5381.L317      331.7'02      77-27010
ISBN 0-8425-0937-2

To

Joyce

# CONTENTS

# ISOLATING
# THE
# PROBLEM

"My son is a junior in high school and has no idea what he would like to do for a living. Do you have a test that will tell him what he should do?"

"My daughter has decided she's sick of school and wants to work a year before going to college. I'm afraid she will never go back. What shall I do?"

"My son is bright but says he has no interest in going to college. How can I make him see how important it is to get a college education?"

"My son is in the eighth grade and has decided he wants to be a policeman. I don't think he would be good at it and I'll bet he wouldn't like it. I really think he has been influenced by *Baretta, Starsky and Hutch,* and other police shows."

"My daughter graduated from college as a psychology major but couldn't get a job. Now she's taking a business course to get a secretarial job. What a waste of time and money! Why didn't someone tell her about the problems she would have finding a job in that field?"

In the last year I've been asked these questions and more by parents of children having difficulty choosing a career. Parents seem to feel helpless to influence or assist their children in making good career choices. Must they feel this way? I think the answer is no.

If you are convinced that making a good career decision is im-

1

portant and that you have a responsibility to help your child in this process, read on.

Career decision making is a developmental process beginning when a person is relatively young and continuing throughout life. It is not a phenomenon that occurs at some magic time in adolescence. The prevailing myth about career decisions goes like this: Between about the ages of sixteen and twenty-four, a person looks at himself or herself and determines what training and skills he or she has. The person is then to look "out there" in the professional world and find a job that uses those skills, making a perfect match. The two, person and career, are joined and live happily ever after. This, however, is not realistic. Most people today will change jobs from four to eight times during their lives. They may need retraining from time to time, no matter what level of job they have, depending on the changes in the labor market and the changes in themselves. We cannot always expect a forty-year-old to be happy with a decision made by an eighteen-year-old.

We will discuss this decision-making process later in the book. You as parents, however, can do certain things to help your children make good career choices, have good work attitudes, and develop good job-seeking and job-holding skills. Let's look for a moment at some of the facets of one's life that are affected by career choice and then discuss some of the things you can do to help your children deal with them.

Career choice affects the geographical area in which one will live. For example, a marine biologist probably won't settle in Tucson, Arizona. That may be obvious, but there are some less obvious realities to be considered. Recently I talked to a group of students in an area where the main industries are chicken processing, tourism, and fishing. The students were discussing what careers they planned to pursue, and their choices were not too different from the choices of students in many other parts of the country. Many wanted to be flight attendants (the desexed title for stewardesses), computer programmers, pilots, lawyers, auto mechanics, and fashion models. However, there was one constraint: none of them wanted to leave the area. They had never looked at the employment outlook in their area for the jobs they wanted to do. I told them, "If you train to be an engineer and end up a chicken plucker, you've made a bad choice. However, if you have carefully thought out the life-style that will give you the most satisfaction wherever you decide to live, and you decide that working in the chicken industry is the best way to achieve that life-style—you've made a good choice. It is not *what* you choose that is so important; it is *how* you arrive at that decision."

A career decision may sometimes affect whom you marry. At one community college, I was working with a group of students, all of whom were in their twenties. One man, a business administration major planning a career in middle management, had already made contact with the local branch of a nationally known firm. They were apparently impressed with him and were encouraging him to finish his degree. They had practically promised him a position. But the company policy was to transfer employees at the middle management level every two years, and the man was engaged to a girl who wanted never to leave her home area. There, then, was a definite problem.

I am not suggesting that young people conduct a career interview before planning marriage, but there should be some discussion of career plans prior to marriage. Many men have given up promotions because their wives did not want to move; many women have given up careers to move with their husbands. You may know of cases where families have split up because of incompatible career plans. With more career options developing for women, this will become more of a problem. Are your children prepared for this? What can you do to help them?

A career decision determines, in some cases, the neighborhood where one will live. This is true for economic reasons as well as for proximity to work. An acquaintance of mine majored in agriculture because he was raised on a farm and enjoyed the outdoors. He also valued security, was competent in his job, and was an achiever. As a result, he was employed by the Department of Agriculture. He now lives in a suburb and has to commute to a city every day, fighting traffic for 45 minutes each way, only to spend eight hours indoors—hardly what he had in mind. Had he been more aware of what he valued in his life-style, would he have chosen differently? Perhaps he would have made a more informed decision.

Career choice is also related to choice of leisure activities. A person making $40,000 a year can, and probably does, enjoy different leisure activities from one who makes $10,000 a year. A person making $10,000 a year may not be able to afford to ski, play golf, go yachting, or go to the legitimate theatre very often.

A construction worker will probably enjoy different leisure activities from a person who sits behind a desk all day.

Many young people enter training in an activity they enjoyed in their leisure time; sometimes this is a good choice and sometimes it is not. One girl I know is a gifted musician and majored in music in college. She is now teaching music in a junior high school and conducting the school's band and chorus, and is less than satisfied with her choice. Teaching, it seems, was a far cry from what she had planned for her life. There are even golf pros who hate their work now that it is their livelihood.

Constructive leisure can help give a person a satisfying life. It can provide the satisfaction that one's job does not; thus, it is important to encourage good use of leisure time. This, too, is influenced by a career choice.

These are random examples of how career decisions can affect other decisions people make. Too often these decisions are made in isolation from each other. Young people must learn that their career will affect their entire life-style. In short, the question, "What do you want to be when you grow up?" is really obsolete. A better question is, "How do you want to live your life and what are several career options that will provide you with that life-style?

To determine the kind of life-style they want and can expect, your children must answer questions such as: Do I want to live in a small town? a suburb? a large city? an isolated area? Do I want to marry? have children? travel on the job? Do I want a job that will take me away from the family for part of the time? Do I want my spouse to stay home and take care of the kids while I work? Most importantly, they must know the answers to these questions: What are my abilities? What are my interests? What do I value?

Most of us have a limited idea of what our skills are. We often overlook or seldom think about the things that come easily to us. We are usually not clear about our values—those things that are really important to us, such as excitement, security, prestige, money, a nice home, the chance to help others, the occasion to make a lasting contribution to society. In choosing a life-style, some compromises may be necessary. Therefore, you as parents can best assist your children by helping them clarify their interests, aptitudes, and values and come up with several career options that will lead to that life-style. This will help them make a compromise, if necessary, that still provides them with a satisfying life.

If your child values money, prestige, and the chance to help others and after exploring the work world decides that becoming a doctor will obtain this life-style, then he or she should be free to consider studying medicine. But, if not accepted into medical school or forced to quit for academic or financial reasons, he or she will be able to adjust to a compromise if other options have been developed.

The following example illustrates the importance of life-style and value considerations in selecting a career. Dan is a federal police officer in Washington, D.C. He works nights patrolling and safeguarding foreign embassies. He likes his job, but wishes he made more money. What keeps him from applying for some higher-paying federal law enforcement job? He says it wouldn't fit in with the way he wants to live his life. "I could finish my degree and qualify for a treasury agent job, but if I got such a job I'd probably have to travel and possibly work undercover for long periods of time. Or I might be assigned to an investigation lasting six months in a place miles away from home. My wife and I have only been married a few years and I don't want to be separated for long periods of time."

Dan gave other reasons for his decision. His wife is a teacher and has a tenured position in the Washington area. "Becoming a federal agent of some sort could mean relocation to another city, and my wife might have trouble getting a job. Our total family income would probably suffer every time I was relocated. There's another reason, too: I'm twenty-eight now, and if I stick with this job another sixteen years I can retire at better than half pay. I'd be only forty-four, and that's young enough to start the second career I really want."

"What is that?"

"I've always been interested in cabinet work. I like doing things with my hands, and since I work nights, I spend many afternoons doing cabinet work. I'm not sure if I'd like to work as an independent cabinet maker, but it's a thought."

You may not want a life-style like Dan's nor share his values nor agree with his decision, but they are his values and life-style, and his decision takes them into account. He values money, but he values nearness to his wife more, so family considerations are a high-ranking value to him. Although Dan might prefer doing cabinet work for a living, he also values security. By compromising, he can work with wood while working at a secure job.

Then at age forty-four, with the financial security of a good pension, he can do what he enjoys full time.

Your children might not come to the same conclusions Dan did, were they in his shoes. But his decision was right for him because that is the way he wants it. Another choice could be the right one for your daughter or son, if that is the way she or he wants it. In the following chapters I will be giving you strategies and exercises as well as ideas to help your child make the best decisions in planning her or his life.

It could be that you, as a parent, are not completely satisfied with your career. These same strategies could assist you in making a mid-career change. More and more middle-aged adults are making career changes. The point of these exercises is to do them as a family, talk about them, and discuss future options. Not only will they provide you and your children with information to help make good decisions, but they can also be fun and helpful in bringing the family closer together.

These exercises have also been used in larger groups made up of people of different ages, such as young adults about to enter the labor market or go to school, older adults wanting to reenter the labor market or change jobs, and those looking forward to retirement. Families with parents in the thirty-five–to–fifty age range are often composed of mothers wanting to reenter the labor market, fathers dissatisfied with their jobs, and teenagers not knowing where to go or what to do. It is possible that you know several families in this same situation—perhaps you would like to join with them in doing these exercises as a group. In any case, give them a try. Good luck!

# 1

## INTERESTS, APTITUDES, AND VALUES

One of the questions asked in the introduction was, "My son is a junior in high school and has no idea what he would like to do. Do you have a test that will tell him what he should do?"

I hear this question or some variation of it at least once a week. Parents with children from fifteen to twenty-five will even pay money to find a foolproof answer to this question with a quick and easy battery of tests. But there is no test battery that will satisfy this requirement. There are tests that will assist young people in clarifying their interests and aptitudes, but these can only give clues as to a wise career choice. Tests of this kind are not definitive and should not be considered so.

In this chapter activities will be presented that will provide you and your children with essentially the same information as would these tests. Before you begin, however, let us find out where you, as parents, stand in your own career awareness. Do not read ahead and do not respond as you think you should. Just let your answers come as they will.

### Activity One

On a piece of paper, quickly write down those jobs that you would consider appropriate for your son or daughter. Now turn the paper over and write on the other side those careers that you would like represented if you were among a group of people stranded on a desert island.

Next, answer these questions:

1.  Do your two lists differ?
2.  Do you consider some careers important but inappropriate for your child? Why?
3.  Are you more interested in seeing your child follow a career satisfying to her or him, or one that will make you proud?
4.  Would your list of careers appropriate for your child be different if his or her sex were different? That is, if you were thinking of your son when you made the list, would it be the same for your daughter?
5.  Do you believe that certain careers are inappropriate for women? What are they and why are they inappropriate?
6.  Do you consider some careers inappropriate for men? What are they and why?
7.  What would your reaction be if your son or daughter chose one of these "inappropriate" careers?
8.  Would you be willing to share the responses to these questions with your children? If so, do it. If not, why not?
9.  Would you be willing to share the responses to these questions with your friends?
10.  Have you really been honest?

This exercise should help make you aware of your attitude toward possible career choices for your daughter or son. If you like the way you responded, fine. If you don't like your responses, at least you are aware of your own bias, and that is the first step to change—if you want to change. These attitudes of yours will affect your children's choices. Your attitudes may be manifested in subtle ways, but they will still be influential. Some children rebel against a parental attitudes, and others go along with their parents' wishes; you probably know which of your children will react in which way.

With a little ingenuity you can modify this activity and have your children participate in it, too. Try it after dinner or on a rainy afternoon. Then share your lists and talk about them. There are no right or wrong answers. For this and the following exercises you will have to decide at what age they would be appropriate for your children. However, they have been found to be effective with people as young as twelve years and as old as forty-five. Since values, interests, and aptitudes change, these exercises can be done more than once as the child grows older. It is a good idea to keep the responses in a folder so that your child or young adult can see how he or she has changed in his or her attitudes.

Another section of this book will deal with the career development of small children and activities appropriate for them. The purpose of exploring careers with young children is not to force them into making early decisions, but rather to make them aware of themselves and of the world of work options open to them. With this awareness, they will not find themselves as seniors in high school saying, "Good grief, I'm graduating this year; what will I do? I guess I'll go to the community college," or "I guess I'll just get a job." Too often young people choose college only to put off making a decision for two or four more years.

The activities related to interests, aptitudes, and values will be interspersed. At the end of this chapter, you and your family will have a much better awareness of yourselves and how these factors relate to your lives. These exercises can be done individually or as a family, but the best results will occur if you do them together as a family.

## Activity Two[1]

(30-45 minutes after dinner)

Each person should have a pencil and a piece of paper (The back of a napkin will do.)

1. Quickly write down ten things you like to do most. Write anything down; you don't have to share anything you don't want to. Write them in a column in no special order. Don't think too long; just quickly write the first things that come into your mind.
2. Place an "X" next to those things you have done within the last 3 weeks.
3. Place an "A" next to those things you like to do alone.
4. Place a "P" next to those things you like to do with people.
5. Place a "$" next to those that cost $5.00 or more each time you do them.
6. Place an "O" next to those you would like to have be a part of your occupation.
7. Place an "L" next to those you would like to have be a part of your leisure.
8. Place an "S" next to those you would like your spouse to have on his or her list.
9. Place an "R" next to those you think you will be able to do after age 60.

9

10. Place an "M" next to those you think your mother would have on her list.

11. Place an "F" next to those you think your father would have on his list.

Each of you should now think of the setting where you would most likely be able to do each of these things (mountains, city, suburb, coast, country, small town, etc.). Each of you may then share your responses and discuss them, emphasizing the question, "What have I learned about myself?" *No one should be forced to share her or his responses.*

### Activity Three

Interests                    (two evenings or two rainy Sunday afternoons)
   Interest inventories are not designed to limit possibilities but to make you aware of some careers you may not have been aware of before. In other words, their purpose is to expand your children's awareness of career possibilities. The careers listed at the end of such an inventory are only a few possibilities to consider.

### JOB-O[2]

What will you be doing a few years from now? What would you like to be doing? How can you find out what you want to do?

   JOB-O will help you find out how you see yourself, what kind of job best fits your interest, what you like to do most, and what training you need to get that job. However, JOB-O does not measure your ability or aptitude to do the task involved in the occupation you will choose. *JOB-O is exploratory only.*

1. On a blank sheet of paper, in the top half-inch, trace or re-copy the following set of lines in the same proportion in which they appear below:

——    ——   ——   ——   ——   ——   ——   ——   ——
   1       2      3      4      5      6      7      8      9

2. Read each question and place your answer's number on the line above the number of the question on the answer sheet you have drawn.

### Question 1:
### How long do you
### want to go to school?

(Select one number and place that number on the answer paper above the line for question 1.)

I want to ...
1.  complete high school.
2.  complete apprenticeship, technical, or special training.
3.  complete a two-year college program.
4.  complete a four-year college program.
5.  complete five or more years of college.

## Question 2:
## What would you like to do?

(Select the group of activities that you would really enjoy doing, those that would make you happy. Place the number of that group above the line for question 2.)

1.  ARTISTIC-LITERARY (art, drama, music, designing, photography, TV, radio, news reporting, law, writing, library work, drafting, etc.)
2.  BUSINESS, CLERICAL, SALES (data processing, accounting, typing, office work, selling, management, etc.)
3.  SOCIAL-PERSONAL SERVICE (social work, teaching, nursing, police, probation, recreation, cosmetology, flight attendant work, food preparation, etc.)
4.  AGRICULTURE-CONSERVATION (wildlife, forestry, farming-ranching, ecology, mining, logging, etc.)
5.  MECHANICAL (construction, repairing, operating equipment, aviation, transportation, assembling, etc.)
6.  SCIENTIFIC (medicine, engineering, mathematics, electronics, etc.)

## Questions 3 through 9:
### For each statement below,
### decide which one of the six answers
### *best* applies to you.
### Be as honest as you can.

(Place the number of that answer above the line for that question on your answer sheet.)

Question 3: I would like a job in which I work with people.

| | | |
|---|---|---|
| 1. usually | 3. sometimes | 5. rarely |
| 2. often | 4. occasionally | 6. never |

Question 4: I would like a job in which I tell other people what to do.

| | | |
|---|---|---|
| 1. usually | 3. sometimes | 5. rarely |
| 2. often | 4. occasionally | 6. never |

Question 5: I would like a job in which I would be close and friendly with people.

1. usually　　　　　3. sometimes　　　　5. rarely
2. often　　　　　　4. occasionally　　　6. never

Question 6: I would like a job in which I would be physically active.

1. usually　　　　　3. sometimes　　　　5. rarely
2. often　　　　　　4. occasionally　　　6. never

Question 7: I would like a job in which I work with my hands.

1. usually　　　　　3. sometimes　　　　5. rarely
2. often　　　　　　4. occasionally　　　6. never

Question 8: I would like a job in which I work with facts, figures, and information and apply them to my job.

1. usually　　　　　3. sometimes　　　　5. rarely
2. often　　　　　　4. occasionally　　　6. never

Question 9: I would like a job in which I could be creative and work with ideas.

1. usually　　　　　3. sometimes　　　　5. rarely
2. often　　　　　　4. occasionally　　　6. never

Now, move your answer paper with the numbers down the following pages, and write down all job titles that match at least five of your choices.

## Job-O Job Finder

| 1 | 2 | 3 | 4 | 5 | 6 | 7 | 8 | 9 | JOB TITLE |
|---|---|---|---|---|---|---|---|---|-----------|
| 4 | 2 | 3-4 | 2-3 | 3-4 | 5-6 | 5-6 | 1-2 | 2-3 | Accountant |
| 3-4 | 2 | 1-2 | 2-3 | 2-3 | 3-4 | 3-4 | 2-3 | 1-2 | Advertising Worker |
| 2 | 5 | 4-5 | 5-6 | 5-6 | 1-2 | 1-2 | | 2-33-4 | Aircraft Mechanic |
| 2-3 | 6 | 3-4 | 1-2 | 4-5 | 5-6 | 5-6 | 1-2 | 3-4 | Air Traffic Controller |
| 1 | 5 | 5-6 | 5-6 | 5-6 | 2-3 | 1-2 | 2-3 | 2-3 | Appliance Service Technician |
| 5 | 1,6 | 2-3 | 1-2 | 3-4 | 3-4 | 1-2 | 1-2 | 1-2 | Architect |
| 1 | 5 | 3-4 | 5-6 | 3-4 | 3-4 | 1-2 | 5-6 | 5-6 | Assembler |
| 2 | 5 | 5-6 | 5-6 | 5-6 | 1-2 | 1-2 | 4-5 | 3-4 | Auto-body Repair Worker |
| 2 | 5 | 5-6 | 5-6 | 5-6 | 2-3 | 1-2 | 2-3 | 3-4 | Auto Mechanic |
| 1 | 5 | 3-4 | 3-4 | 3-4 | 2-3 | 3-4 | 1-2 | 2-3 | Auto Parts Worker |
| 1 | 2 | 1-2 | 1-2 | 1-2 | 4-5 | 5-6 | 2-3 | 3-4 | Auto Salesperson |
| 1 | 2 | 3-4 | 4-5 | 3-4 | 3-4 | 4-5 | 1-2 | 4-5 | Bank Clerk, Teller |
| 4 | 2 | 1-2 | 1-2 | 1-2 | 3-4 | 4-5 | 1-2 | 1-2 | Bank Officer |
| 2 | 3 | 2-3 | 5-6 | 2-3 | 2-3 | 1-2 | 4-5 | 4-5 | Barber |
| 2-3 | 2 | 3-4 | 5-6 | 3-4 | 5-6 | 5-6 | 1-2 | 5-6 | Bookkeeper |
| 2-3 | 5 | 5-6 | 5-6 | 5-6 | 3-4 | 1-2 | 1-2 | 2-3 | Broadcast Technician |

# Job-O Job Finder

| 1 | 2 | 3 | 4 | 5 | 6 | 7 | 8 | 9 | JOB TITLE |
|---|---|---|---|---|---|---|---|---|-----------|
| 1 | 5 | 5-6 | 5-6 | 2-3 | 1-2 | 1-2 | 2-3 | 2-3 | Bus. Machine Service Technician |
| 2 | 5 | 3-4 | 4-5 | 3-4 | 1-2 | 1-2 | 3-4 | 3-4 | Carpenter |
| 1 | 2 | 3-4 | 5-6 | 3-4 | 3-4 | 3-4 | 3-4 | 5-6 | Cashier |
| 5 | 3 | 1-2 | 1-2 | 1-2 | 3-4 | 5-6 | 2-3 | 2-3 | Clergy |
| 5 | 3 | 1-2 | 1-2 | 3-4 | 5-6 | 5-6 | 1-2 | 1-2 | College Teacher |
| 3-4 | 1 | 3-4 | 3-4 | 3-4 | 4-5 | 1-2 | 3-4 | 1-2 | Commercial Artist |
| 2-3 | 2 | 5-6 | 5-6 | 5-6 | 5-6 | 3-4 | 1-2 | 4-5 | Computer Operator |
| 1-2 | 3 | 3-4 | 3-4 | 3-4 | 2-3 | 2-3 | 3-4 | 3-4 | Cook, Chef |
| 2-3 | 3 | 2-3 | 3-4 | 1-2 | 2-3 | 1-2 | 5-6 | 1-2 | Cosmetologist |
| 4-5 | 3 | 1-2 | 3-4 | 1-2 | 5-6 | 5-6 | 1-2 | 1-2 | Counselor |
| 1 | 3 | 3-4 | 5-6 | 3-4 | 2-3 | 3-4 | 4-5 | 4-5 | Custodian |
| 2-3 | 3 | 3-4 | 5-6 | 3-4 | 3-4 | 3-4 | 4-5 | 5-6 | Dental Assistant |
| 3-4 | 6 | 2-3 | 3-4 | 3-4 | 3-4 | 1-2 | 2-3 | 3-4 | Dental Hygienist |
| 2-3 | 5 | 5-6 | 5-6 | 5-6 | 3-4 | 1-2 | 3-4 | 3-4 | Dental Technician |
| 5 | 6 | 1-2 | 1-2 | 1-2 | 2-3 | 1-2 | 1-2 | 1-2 | Dentist |
| 4 | 6 | 3-4 | 1-2 | 3-4 | 3-4 | 4-5 | 1-2 | 2-3 | Dietitian |
| 2-3 | 1 | 5-6 | 5-6 | 5-6 | 5-6 | 1-2 | 2-3 | 3-4 | Drafter |
| 2 | 5 | 4-5 | 4-5 | 4-5 | 1-2 | 1-2 | 2-3 | 4-5 | Electrician |
| 5 | 3 | 1-2 | 1-2 | 1-2 | 4-5 | 3-4 | 1-2 | 1-2 | Elementary Teacher |
| 4-5 | 6 | 3-4 | 1-2 | 3-4 | 3-4 | 3-4 | 1-2 | 1-2 | Engineer |
| 2-3 | 5-6 | 3-4 | 3-4 | 3-4 | 2-3 | 2-3 | 2-3 | 3-4 | Engineer Technician |
| 4-5 | 4,6 | 3-4 | 3-4 | 3-4 | 3-4 | 3-4 | 1-2 | 1-2 | Environmental Scientist |
| 1 | 3 | 3-4 | 3-4 | 3-4 | 1-2 | 3-4 | 3-4 | 5-6 | Firefighter |
| 4 | 4 | 3-4 | 3-4 | 3-4 | 1-2 | 4-5 | 1-2 | 3-4 | Forester |
| 2-3 | 4 | 3-4 | 5-6 | 3-4 | 1-2 | 4-5 | 3-4 | 5-6 | Forestry Aide |
| 2-3 | 5 | 4-5 | 4-5 | 4-5 | 1-2 | 1-2 | 2-3 | 3-4 | Heating, Air Mechanic |
| 4 | 3 | 1-2 | 2-3 | 2-3 | 3-4 | 3-4 | 1-2 | 1-2 | Home Economist |
| 5 | 2 | 1-2 | 1-2 | 3-4 | 4-5 | 5-6 | 1-2 | 1-2 | Hospital Adminstrator |
| 1 | 3 | 3-4 | 5-6 | 3-4 | 2-3 | 4-5 | 5-6 | 5-6 | Hospital Attendant |
| 1 | 3 | 3-4 | 5-6 | 3-4 | 5-6 | 5-6 | 3-4 | 5-6 | Hotel Clerk |
| 3-4 | 2 | 2-3 | 1-2 | 2-3 | 4-5 | 5-6 | 1-2 | 2-3 | Hotel Manager |
| 2-3 | 6 | 3-4 | 5-6 | 3-4 | 3-4 | 3-4 | 3-4 | 4-5 | Inhalation Technician |
| 1-2 | 5 | 4-5 | 5-6 | 3-4 | 3-4 | 1-2 | 3-4 | 3-4 | Instrument Repair Technician |
| 3-4 | 2 | 1-2 | 1-2 | 1-2 | 5-6 | 5-6 | 2-3 | 3-4 | Insurance Agent |
| 3-4 | 1 | 3-4 | 1-2 | 3-4 | 3-4 | 3-4 | 1-2 | 1-2 | Interior Decorator |
| 2 | 5 | 5-6 | 5-6 | 5-6 | 1-2 | 1-2 | 4-5 | 3-4 | Iron Worker |
| 2-3 | 6 | 3-4 | 5-6 | 3-4 | 3-4 | 1-2 | 1-2 | 3-4 | Lab Technician |
| 5 | 1 | 1-2 | 1-2 | 3-4 | 5-6 | 5-6 | 1-2 | 1-2 | Lawyer |
| 5 | 1 | 1-2 | 3-4 | 3-4 | 4-5 | 5-6 | 1-2 | 1-2 | Librarian |

13

# Job-O Job Finder

| 1 | 2 | 3 | 4 | 5 | 6 | 7 | 8 | 9 | JOB TITLE |
|---|---|---|---|---|---|---|---|---|---|
| 1-3 | 1 | 2-3 | 3-4 | 3-4 | 3-4 | 3-4 | 2-3 | 3-4 | Library Technician |
| 4-5 | 6 | 3-4 | 2-3 | 3-4 | 3-4 | 2-3 | 1-2 | 1-2 | Life Scientist |
| 2 | 1 | 5-6 | 5-6 | 5-6 | 2-3 | 1-2 | 2-3 | 2-3 | Lithographer |
| 1 | 4 | 5-6 | 5-6 | 5-6 | 1-2 | 1-2 | 5-6 | 5-6 | Lumber Worker |
| 2 | 5 | 5-6 | 5-6 | 5-6 | 2-3 | 1-2 | 2-3 | 2-3 | Machinist |
| 1 | 3 | 3-4 | 5-6 | 3-4 | 1-2 | 5-6 | 3-4 | 5-6 | Mail Carrier |
| 3-4 | 2 | 2-3 | 3-4 | 2-3 | 3-4 | 5-6 | 2-3 | 2-3 | Manufacturers Salesperson |
| 4-5 | 2 | 1-2 | 1-2 | 3-4 | 3-4 | 4-5 | 1-2 | 1-2 | Marketing Research Worker |
| 4-5 | 6 | 5-6 | 3-4 | 5-6 | 5-6 | 5-6 | 1-2 | 1-2 | Mathematician |
| 2 | 5 | 3-4 | 5-6 | 4-5 | 1-2 | 1-2 | 4-5 | 5-6 | Meat Cutter |
| 2-3 | 2 | 2-3 | 4-5 | 3-4 | 3-4 | 3-4 | 4-5 | 4-5 | Medical Assistant |
| 4-5 | 6 | 4-5 | 4-5 | 4-5 | 3-4 | 1-2 | 2-3 | 3-4 | Medical Technologist |
| 2 | 1 | 3-4 | 5-6 | 2-3 | 2-3 | 5-6 | 5-6 | 3-4 | Model |
| 3-4 | 1 | 1-2 | 3-4 | 3-4 | 3-4 | 5-6 | 1-2 | 1-2 | Newspaper Reporter |
| 3-4 | 3,6 | 1-2 | 2-3 | 1-2 | 2-3 | 3-4 | 1-2 | 1-2 | Nurse RN |
| 4-5 | 3 | 1-2 | 1-2 | 1-2 | 3-4 | 1-2 | 1-2 | 1-2 | Occupational Therapist |
| 1-2 | 2 | 3-4 | 5-6 | 4-5 | 4-5 | 2-3 | 2-3 | 4-5 | Office Machine Operator |
| 2 | 5 | 5-6 | 5-6 | 5-6 | 1-2 | 3-4 | 5-6 | 5-6 | Operating Engineer |
| 5 | 6 | 1-2 | 1-2 | 3-4 | 3-4 | 1-2 | 1-2 | 1-2 | Optometrist |
| 2 | 5 | 4-5 | 5-6 | 5-6 | 1-2 | 1-2 | 4-5 | 3-4 | Painter |
| 2,4 | 1 | 1-2 | 2-3 | 2-3 | 2-3 | 2-3 | 2-3 | 1-2 | Performing Artist |
| 4 | 3 | 1-2 | 1-2 | 1-2 | 4-5 | 5-6 | 1-2 | 3-4 | Personnel Worker |
| 5 | 6 | 3-4 | 3-4 | 3-4 | 3-4 | 2-3 | 1-2 | 1-2 | Pharmacist |
| 2-3 | 1 | 3-4 | 3-4 | 3-4 | 3-4 | 1-2 | 3-4 | 1-2 | Photograher |
| 4-5 | 6 | 4-5 | 2-3 | 4-5 | 4-5 | 4-5 | 1-2 | 1-2 | Physical Scientist |
| 4-5 | 3 | 1-2 | 1-2 | 1-2 | 2-3 | 1-2 | 1-2 | 2-3 | Physical Therapist |
| 5 | 6 | 1-2 | 1-2 | 1-2 | 2-3 | 1-2 | 1-2 | 1-2 | Physician |
| 3-4 | 6 | 3-4 | 1-2 | 3-4 | 3-4 | 3-4 | 1-2 | 3-4 | Pilot |
| 2 | 5 | 4-5 | 4-5 | 4-5 | 1-2 | 1-2 | 3-4 | 3-4 | Plumber |
| 1,3 | 3 | 1-2 | 1-2 | 1-2 | 1-2 | 5-6 | 2-3 | 4-5 | Police Officer |
| 1 | 2 | 3-4 | 5-6 | 3-4 | 3-4 | 3-4 | 3-4 | 5-6 | Postal Clerk |
| 4 | 3 | 1-2 | 1-2 | 1-2 | 5-6 | 5-6 | 1-2 | 3-4 | Probation Officer |
| 3-4 | 2,6 | 5-6 | 3-4 | 4-5 | 5-6 | 5-6 | 1-2 | 1-2 | Programmer |
| 5 | 3,6 | 1-2 | 1-2 | 1-2 | 5-6 | 5-6 | 1-2 | 1-2 | Psychologist |
| 4 | 2 | 1-2 | 1-2 | 1-2 | 5-6 | 5-6 | 1-2 | 1-2 | Public Relations Worker |
| 3-4 | 2 | 2-3 | 2-3 | 3-4 | 5-6 | 5-6 | 1-2 | 3-4 | Purchasing Agent |
| 2-3 | 2 | 1-2 | 1-2 | 1-2 | 3-4 | 5-6 | 3-4 | 3-4 | Real Estate Salesperson |
| 1 | 3 | 2-3 | 3-4 | 2-3 | 4-5 | 4-5 | 3-4 | 4-5 | Receptionist |
| 3-4 | 3 | 1-2 | 1-2 | 1-2 | 1-2 | 3-4 | 2-3 | 2-3 | Recreation Worker |

14

# Job-O Job Finder

| 1 | 2 | 3 | 4 | 5 | 6 | 7 | 8 | 9 | JOB TITLE |
|---|---|---|---|---|---|---|---|---|---|
| 1 | 2 | 3-4 | 5-6 | 3-4 | 3-4 | 5-6 | 3-4 | 5-6 | Retail Salesperson |
| 4 | 6 | 3-4 | 3-4 | 3-4 | 3-4 | 3-4 | 2-3 | 2-3 | Sanitarian |
| 5 | 3 | 1-2 | 1-2 | 1-2 | 4-5 | 5-6 | 1-2 | 1-2 | Secondary Teacher |
| 2-3 | 2 | 2-3 | 3-4 | 2-3 | 5-6 | 3-4 | 2-3 | 3-4 | Secretary |
| 4 | 2 | 1-2 | 1-2 | 1-2 | 5-6 | 5-6 | 1-2 | 1-2 | Securities Salesperson |
| 1 | 5 | 3-4 | 5-6 | 3-4 | 2-3 | 3-4 | 5-6 | 5-6 | Service Station Attendant |
| 1 | 2 | 4-5 | 5-6 | 4-5 | 1-2 | 3-4 | 3-4 | 4-5 | Shipping/Receiving Clerk |
| 5 | 3,6 | 3,6 | 3-4 | 1-2 | 4-5 | 5-6 | 1-2 | 1-2 | Social Scientist |
| 4-5 | 3 | 1-2 | 1-2 | 1-2 | 3-4 | 5-6 | 1-2 | 1-2 | Social Worker |
| 5 | 3 | 3-4 | 3-4 | 2-3 | 4-5 | 4-5 | 3-4 | 2-3 | Speech Pathologist – |
| 5 | 6 | 4-5 | 3-4 | 4-5 | 5-6 | 5-6 | 1-2 | 1-2 | Statistician |
| 2-3 | 3 | 1-2 | 2-3 | 2-3 | 2-3 | 5-6 | 3-4 | 3-4 | Stewardess, Steward |
| 1,3 | 4,6 | 3-4 | 3-4 | 3-4 | 2-3 | 2-3 | 1-2 | 3-4 | Surveyor |
| 4 | 6 | 3-4 | 1-2 | 3-4 | 5-6 | 5-6 | 1-2 | 1-2 | Systems Analyst |
| 4 | 1,6 | 3-4 | 3-4 | 3-4 | 5-6 | 5-6 | 1-2 | 1-2 | Technical Writer |
| 1 | 5 | 5-6 | 5-6 | 5-6 | 1-2 | 1-2 | 3-4 | 4-5 | Telephone Crafts Technician |
| 1 | 2 | 5-6 | 5-6 | 5-6 | 1-2 | 1-2 | 3-4 | 4-5 | Telephone Operator |
| 1 | 5 | 5-6 | 5-6 | 5-6 | 2-3 | 3-4 | 3-4 | 5-6 | Truck, Bus Driver |
| 1-2 | 5 | 3-4 | 4-5 | 4-5 | 3-4 | 1-2 | 1-2 | 2-3 | TV/Radio Service Technician |
| 1 | 2 | 4-5 | 5-6 | 5-6 | 5-6 | 2-3 | 4-5 | 5-6 | Typist |
| 5 | 3 | 1-2 | 1-2 | 3-4 | 3-4 | 5-6 | 1-2 | 1-2 | Urban Planner |
| 5 | 4,6 | 3-4 | 1-2 | 3-4 | 2-3 | 1-2 | 1-2 | 1-2 | Veterinarian |
| 2-3 | 3 | 1-2 | 3-4 | 1-2 | 2-3 | 3-4 | 3-4 | 3-4 | Vocational Nurse |
| 2-3 | 5 | 5-6 | 5-6 | 5-6 | 1-2 | 1-2 | 3-4 | 3-4 | Welder |
| 1,3 | 2 | 3-4 | 3-4 | 3-4 | 4-5 | 5-6 | 2-3 | 4-5 | Wholesale Salesperson |
| 2-3 | 6 | 4-5 | 3-4 | 4-5 | 3-4 | 3-4 | 1-2 | 4-5 | X-Ray Technologist |

Find some hilarious surprises? Perhaps, mother, you can't imagine yourself as an operating engineer? There will undoubtedly be some jobs you or your children will not think suitable. However, you may not really be aware of what people in those jobs really do, or you may have stereotyped ideas of what they do.

List the three from your list that appeal to you the most; later on, you can research them to find out more about them. This doesn't mean that you are suited for any of these jobs. It is just a beginning.

15

## Activity Four

(30 minutes to 1 hour)

### *Values in a Nutshell*[3]

On a piece of paper draw your nutshell similar to the one below. Now follow the instructions as to what to place in each of the sections.

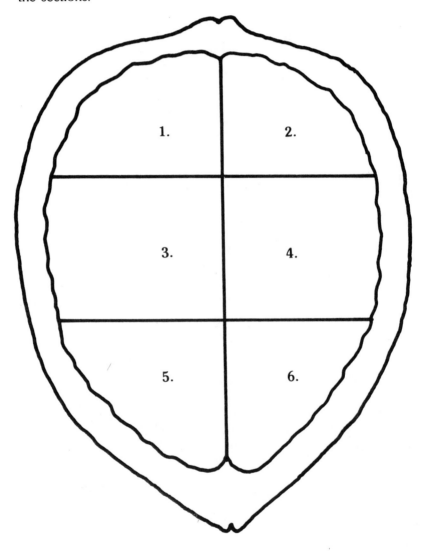

### Section 1.
### Draw a picture of yourself
### doing two things you do well.

Examples:     driving, cooking

### Section 2.
### Draw a picture of the one thing
### you have done in your life
### of which you are most proud.

Examples:     getting a promotion, getting a high school diploma

### Section 3.
### Write down two of your values
### that you would not give up
### under any circumstances.

Examples:     honesty, faithfulness to friends

### Section 4.
### Write down two qualities
### or character traits that you
### would like to develop.

Examples:     outgoing, rich, friendly

### Section 5.
### Write down the project that
### you would undertake today
### if you were guaranteed success
### in one year.

Examples:     paint a picture, build a house

### Section 6.
### Write down the two things that
### you would like to overhear
### someone say about you—things
### that would make you feel good.

Examples:     "She is a person you can trust." "He is so talented in music."

These are your values in a nutshell. Each person in your family should have an opportunity to share each part of his or her responses. On the other hand, no one should be forced to respond to any item. Parents should not place their values on anyone else's responses. Saying "good" to some and saying nothing to others, or simply changing a facial expression, can be interpreted as approval or disapproval. Values are very personal, and each child should feel free to express her or his own. Try asking the question, "What have you learned about yourself that you were not aware of before?"

Now go back to the nutshell and circle numbers one, two, and five. These three areas could be considered somewhat applicable to career choice. This does not mean that they definitely are, but that they could be. The other sections could represent values that might be incompatible with certain careers. For example, if security is a value your son would not relinquish, then there are some careers he would not choose—such as that of a seasonal laborer who only works summers. If hearing someone say, "She is a sweet person" is important to your daughter, then there are some careers she should not choose. Any career where she must maintain tight control over the actions of others is not likely to yield much praise from coworkers. Careers should be investigated in terms of one's values before a choice is made.

Now let us look at aptitudes and skills.

## Activity Five

### *What Have I Done in My Life?*

(One to several hours)

Each family member writes in detail some particular excerpt from his or her life. This should include, in detail, everything that the person did at that time. For instance, if it concerns a job that the person had, it should not just say, "I babysat." The details of everything that was done in that babysitting job should be included. If the mother is a housewife, she should list everything she does as a housewife. It should also include all leisure pursuits. After this is done, one family member should read his or her excerpt aloud, while the other family members write down all the skills that are demonstrated in that excerpt. Then each member

18

reads off the list of skills noted for that person. These can then be discussed. Each family member in turn reads her or his excerpt, following the same procedure.

Here is an example of an excerpt:

At age twenty-two, I was without work—I could not get a teaching job because of the surplus of teachers in southern California. I was broke and needed a job until I could find something related to my training. I was depressed. I happened to see a "help wanted" sign in a cafeteria and decided to go in.

"We need someone to make and serve coffee in the cafeteria line. Can you make coffee?"

"Sure," I said, hoping there were directions on the can or coffee maker since I had never made coffee in my life. But I was willing to try—what did I have to lose? I was to be paid the minimum wage.

The job turned out to be easy for me. I had to measure the coffee into the coffee maker, fill it with water, and plug it in. I also had to order coffee when we were about to run out. I had to keep my area clean and clean out the pot at the end of each day. I also had to put cream in the coffee, if the customer wanted it, and make tea.

We had a lot of older people eating in the cafeteria. I used to chat with them and soon began to recognize returning customers and remember how they wanted their coffee. I learned that Mrs. Jones liked Boston coffee (half cream and half coffee) and that Mr. Smith wanted me to put just a dab of hot water in his coffee, and so on. The customers felt good that I remembered what they wanted.

In two weeks, I was promoted to short-order cook. In this position I had to cook hamburgers, steaks, cheeseburgers, eggs, hash browns, and other short-order items. I also had to clean the grill and give orders to those who made cold sandwiches. Again I learned that Mr. Jones liked a hamburger well done without a bun, and so forth, and continued to chat with customers.

One day, a woman asked me if I was satisfied being a cook. I told her of my plight. She turned out to be a friend of the superintendent of schools in a small community in Los Angeles county.

## Sample Skill Identification:

1. willing to take a risk

2. enthusiastic

3. social skills

4. good memory

5. willing to please

6. ambitious

7. didn't get discouraged

8. good self-concept

9. analytical skill (knew when to order coffee)

10. willing to learn

11. not afraid to work at jobs not using his training

12. creative

13. administrative skills (gave orders)

14. conscientious, friendly, etc.

You may question the listing of some of these things as skills. They are, though, since *every* one of them is marketable in certain circumstances. There are three types of skills. All of these are demonstrated in this excerpt.

1. *Formally acquired skills*—those that were learned in school or another training institution. Generally we have the highest regard for these skills because we worked hardest to acquire them.

2. *Informally acquired skills*—those we learn on the job or in daily living. These are normally valued somewhat less than the ones formally acquired because they came easier.

3. *Naturally acquired skills*—those skills we were either born with or acquired when very young. In most cases we do not even consider these skills because they are so natural to us. Instead, the naturally acquired skills should be considered of greatest value because they come so easy to us and we enjoy doing them the most. In a job the naturally acquired skills will probably give us the greatest satisfaction.

Go back over your excerpts. Have you forgotten any skills, especially naturally acquired ones? They are important when making a career choice.

You can do this exercise over and over again, using different excerpts from your lives. The more often you try it, the better you will know what skills you and your children have. You can then begin to categorize your skills in terms of those you enjoy doing, those you feel neutral about, and those you dislike.

A child who is twelve years old can write an excerpt of a happening at school or at play in his or her recent past, or something that happened in the first grade or before. If he or she was given a responsibility in school, Scouts, church, or whatever, this can be used for skill identification with the family's help. This is not only a valuable experience to identify skills but is good for developing a positive self-concept in young children. It is also fun. It can be enjoyable at a party as a get-acquainted activity.

## Activity Six

### (1 hour)

This activity will assist all of the family in looking at values related to the work place itself. Remember that the value of all these exercises lies in the sharing and discussion that occurs afterwards.

## *What Are Your Work Values?*

Ideas about the characteristics of a desirable work place vary greatly. What are your work values? The following inventory consists of twenty items, each describing the two extremes of a major work characteristic: e.g., work with people vs. work alone. For each item, check the space which best describes your own values.

|  | Very Important | Moderately Important | Not Important |
|---|---|---|---|
| Work for organization | _____ | _____ | _____ |
| Work alone | _____ | _____ | _____ |
| Structured environment: well-defined duties and responsibilities | _____ | _____ | _____ |
| Close supervision | _____ | _____ | _____ |
| Low level of responsibility: no critical decisions | _____ | _____ | _____ |
| Short hours: maximum eight hours per day | _____ | _____ | _____ |
| Guaranteed regular hours | _____ | _____ | _____ |
| Variety of duties every day | _____ | _____ | _____ |
| Challenges and risks in work | _____ | _____ | _____ |
| Fast pace, high pressure | _____ | _____ | _____ |
| Visible end products: specific achievable goals | _____ | _____ | _____ |
| Work indoors in pleasant environment | _____ | _____ | _____ |
| Willing to relocate anywhere | _____ | _____ | _____ |
| Work for large business | _____ | _____ | _____ |
| High prestige and status | _____ | _____ | _____ |
| Many opportunities for advancement and professional development | _____ | _____ | _____ |
| Live close to work | _____ | _____ | _____ |
| Close work with machines | _____ | _____ | _____ |
| Early retirement | _____ | _____ | _____ |
| Frequent travel | _____ | _____ | _____ |

| Not Important | Moderately Important | Very Important | |
|---|---|---|---|
| _____ | _____ | _____ | Self-employment |
| _____ | _____ | _____ | Work with other people |
| _____ | _____ | _____ | Unstructured work: room for creativity and initiative |
| _____ | _____ | _____ | No supervision |
| _____ | _____ | _____ | High level of responsibility: make key decisions |
| _____ | _____ | _____ | Long hours and week-end work usual |
| _____ | _____ | _____ | Possible overtime |
| _____ | _____ | _____ | Similar duties every day |
| _____ | _____ | _____ | Security offered in work |
| _____ | _____ | _____ | Slow pace, low pressure |
| _____ | _____ | _____ | Can't see results of work: long-range goals |
| _____ | _____ | _____ | Work outdoors in all weather and conditions |
| _____ | _____ | _____ | Work in specific geographical area |
| _____ | _____ | _____ | Work for small business |
| _____ | _____ | _____ | Low prestige and status |
| _____ | _____ | _____ | Few opportunities for advancement and professional development |
| _____ | _____ | _____ | Live half-hour or more from work |
| _____ | _____ | _____ | Little work with machines |
| _____ | _____ | _____ | Work opportunities after 65 |
| _____ | _____ | _____ | Little or no travel |

23

Do not bore yourselves and your children by going through these exercises one right after another. There is some value in having a rest period between them. Sometimes you may think of things as a result of an exercise; if so, talk about them, and encourage your children to do the same. Do not try to show that your responses are best; just listen to the children. If you have changed an idea as a result of what they have shared, let them know about it—it will make them feel good. Do not take yourself too seriously.

Above all, have a good time when you do these activities. Do not lecture or moralize. If any of you tire of doing them, stop for awhile. Be creative in ways to introduce each activity. Keep it fun and interesting.

There are many ways of discovering aptitudes and interests, some more informal than others. Here is another instrument that assists children in assessing both aptitudes and interests.

## Activity Seven

### *Self-Appraisal and Assessment Structure* [4]

Each of the following twelve scales includes seven numbered paragraphs. Each paragraph describes a degree of performance in the *field* or *level* being rated. Read each scale carefully, compare each of the paragraphs with your own abilities, and then choose the one that seems to fit you best. Interests as well as abilities are important. Following the four *level* scales is a device by which you can indicate your interest in each of the eight fields.

As you read the seven steps in a scale, you may find that none of the paragraphs fits you exactly. If a paragraph were written to fit you exactly, it would fit no one else. Each paragraph is written to describe a certain degree of ability; you are asked to find the paragraph that comes closest to describing what you can do. You may find that you have trouble in choosing between two paragraphs because each has some statements that refer to you and others that do not. At this point, try to choose the one that comes closest to describing activities you can do or could do if you had the opportunity.

As you study each of the scales, you will note that one, two, or three sentences in each paragraph are italicized. You will save time if you read only the italicized sentence first. Then, when

24

you must choose between one or two or three paragraphs, read the paragraphs being considered in entirety.

## Scientific Field

Study the seven ratings carefully. Each rating lists a number of activities that illustrate a degree of performance. You may not do all the things listed in any of the paragraphs. However, choose the paragraph that lists activities that come closest to resembling your own. After you have chosen the rating that describes you best, turn to the Profile Sheet and record your rating.

1. *I can read compasses, dials on machines, and gauges. I am able to tell the temperature by reading a thermometer.* I can clean laboratory equipment and can follow health and safety rules if they are explained to me.

2. *I can understand the more obvious science demonstrations but have trouble with those that require explanations. If given clear directions, I can care for lab equipment.* I can learn from class discussion but have trouble with most science books.

3. *I have some understanding of natural laws and scientific principles. Although I can get some science information from books, most of what I learn comes from talks and explanations by teachers.* I learn from experiments performed by the teacher but have trouble setting up experiments of my own.

4. *I have average scientific abilities. I can perform basic experiments and can work fundamental problems in science. My understanding of scientific principles is average but no more.* I do not participate in any scientific activities beyond those required for my school assignments.

5. *My science abilities are good. Although I do very little science reading on my own, I do more than is required in my school science courses. My hobbies include some science activity.* I am able to perform and understand the majority of the assigned experiments. I can work the basic science problems and have a general understanding of the fundamental laws.

6. *My scientific activities go beyond required school performance. I read books and articles of a scientific and technical nature that have no direct relationship to my science assignments.* I can work all but the most difficult problems and can understand and perform all assigned experiments. My hobbies have included science collections and airplane and automobile models.

*7. My scientific abilities are such that I am able to perform experiments and conduct research on my own. I have prepared displays for science fairs and school science exhibits. I have good understanding of the theoretical aspects of science and keep abreast of recent scientific and technical developments.* I am able to volunteer to class discussions or discussions with my science teachers concepts and information that supplement the textbook or class reference books. I participate in out-of-school scientific discussions sponsored by science groups or colleges.

## Mechanical Field

Study the seven ratings carefully and, using the same procedures described on the Scientific scale, choose the paragraph that fits you. Record your rating on the profile.

1. *I am able to load a camera, hammer a nail, drive a car, or operate a buffer or vacuum cleaner.* I can use simple mechanical tools.

2. *I am able to operate motors. I understand how most simple machines (pulleys, gears, electric bells) work but am not able to make repairs.* I can use hand tools for ordinary labor-type jobs. I am able to paint and maintain machines or buildings.

3. *Although I don't spend much time trying to repair mechanical objects, I can make minor repairs. I seldom am able to figure out how mechanical objects or puzzles work.* I have fair coordination and can work reasonably well with my hands. As a result, I can perform easy mechanical tasks. I can operate a sewing machine.

4. *I can make repairs and am able to understand the workings of most mechanical toys and simple machines. I can make three-dimensional drawings of regularly shaped objects.* I can use hand tools effectively and can handle the simpler power tools. I can make minor repairs on a car, or I am able to sew, knit, or crochet skillfully.

5. *I am good at mechanics. I often repair implements and toys around the house. I have built numerous model cars and/or airplanes. The mechanical principles involved in conventional machines do not baffle me.* I have good spatial relations and hand-finger dexterity. I am good at mechanical drawing and often make scaled drawings prior to building a mechanical object. I can use a pattern to sew a garment and have on occasion modified patterns. I can tear down and reassemble an automobile engine.

6. *My mechanical abilities are strong. I am skilled in taking things apart, putting them together, and solving mechanical puzzles. I am a good math student. My hobbies include radio, chess, and/or hi-fi.* I can design and make my own clothes, design and build hot-rods, or design and produce jewelry or other ornaments. I understand the basic fundamentals of radio, television, and electronics.

7. *I have a tremendous curiosity about what makes things work. I do much reading on theoretical mechanics. I can improvise, design, and/or improve mechanical devices. I am an excellent math student and can apply my mathematical knowledge to mechanical applications.* I have been a member of my school math team, have participated in math contests, am a ham operator, and produce model computers and/or models of testing machines. I collect stamps or coins and am a good chess player.

## Clerical Field

Study the seven ratings carefully and choose the paragraph that fits you.

1. *With supervision, I can check tools or other objects in and out of storage areas. I can be depended on to deliver messages by hand or by telephone.* I can stuff envelopes with letters and am able to staple papers together to produce pamphlets.

2. *I can catalogue articles according to simple directions and can check articles in and out of storage areas. I cannot, however, make accurate recordings as I cannot spell well or write clear and meaningful reports.* Routine work doesn't bother me and as a result I can do the same task over and over.

3. *I can hear well enough to follow directions given by my teachers, and my eyesight is good. I am able to put words in alphabetical order and numbers in numerical order.* Doing routine and repetitive work does not bore me. Although my work is readable, it is not very neat. I type slowly and make many errors.

4. *I can take directions fairly well and am able to carry out clearly expressed instructions or orders. I am able to find words or numbers that are out of a pre-chosen order or sequence.* I work skillfully with my fingers, and my hand-eye coordination is good. I can copy accurately and am able to take care of details. I am a good typist.

5. *My spelling skills are good and I can write well-constructed*

paragraphs. *I can take directions graciously. I can meet people well and am able to converse satisfactorily. My written papers are neat and accurate.* I have nimble fingers, have a good sense of rhythm, and am an accurate and rapid typist. I can detect words that have been misspelled or improperly used.

6. *I spell accurately and am able to write correctly. My composition and grammar skills are excellent. I am able to organize my time and activities well. I work with written materials rapidly and accurately.* I have good eyesight, excellent hearing, and excellent finger dexterity and hand coordination. I can work well with my fellow students and often do more than is expected of me. I am a fast and accurate typist and my work is neat and attractive.

7. *I am not only able to organize my own time and activities well and do the tasks listed above, but can plan and organize the activities of others as well. My typing speed and accuracy are excellent.* I can read reports, letters, and themes of other students and correct them so that the spelling, punctuation, and sequence of sentences or paragraphs are improved where necessary. I not only take directions well but am able to give directions to others without irritating them. I can make decisions quickly. I am active in Junior Achievement, business clubs, etc.

### Computational Field

Study the seven ratings carefully and choose the paragraph that fits you.

1. *I can add and subtract whole numbers. While I can solve problems in number form (25–21 = 4), I am not able to work word problems.* (I had fifteen dollars and earned twenty dollars. If I then spent twenty-five dollars, how much money did I have left?)

2. *My main difficulties with arithmetic are due to a lack of accuracy. I make many small and foolish mistakes. I can multiply and do short division.* I do not know how to make or keep a budget.

3. *Although I make an occasional error, I know my arithmetic fundamentals (addition, subtraction, multiplication, and division). I can solve most general math problems.* I can make change without making errors.

4. *I have fairly good abilities in working with numbers and in keeping records. I can usually tell when words or numbers that should be in some kind of order are out of place.* I can successfully convert feet to inches, ounces to pounds, and minutes to seconds.

5. *I have good command of arithmetic fundamentals. Decimals and fractions do not baffle me. I am orderly and can and do budget my time and money.* I am able to convert meters to feet, know how to read and produce graphs and tables, and can compute percent and interest.

6. *I find that "a place for everything and everything in its place" is a motto that fits my pattern of operation. I can work with figures for long periods of time without becoming bored.* I understand and can compute compound interest and can convert time from one time zone to another. I am a stickler for accuracy and detail and do my work in a neat, logical, and orderly manner.

7. *When I see numbers on a form in an area of interest, I am not comfortable until I know what they mean. I can find my way through statistical and financial reports. I can utilize tables, charts, and graphs to produce neat, concise reports.* I am able to make out budgets, find and correct computational errors, and make statistical studies. I am able to understand and get pleasure from such activities as computing batting averages; figuring golf, bowling, and racing handicaps; studying the stock market; planning usage for simple computers; and playing number puzzles and games.

### Sales Field

Study the seven ratings carefully and choose the paragraph that fits you.

1. *I enjoy being by myself and make friends slowly. If I worked in a store, I would be more successful working by myself than waiting on customers.*

2. *I stay away from groups as much as possible and when I do get in a group, I usually listen. If I do make a comment, it is to one or two friends.* I have trouble speaking in class. Talking friends into doing things that I want to do is hard. I can wait on customers who have already decided what they are going to buy.

3. *I have a few close friends but cannot say that I influence many people. I do not join many clubs or take part in group activities.* I can talk informally in class and can make short talks. I have worked or could work as a gasoline station attendant or dime-store clerk.

4. *I would have no trouble talking to one or two people for the purpose of selling them on an idea or on my candidacy for an*

*office. On the other hand, I would be hard pressed to stand be-*
*fore a group and ask them to vote for me for an office.* I can sell
cookies at a bake sale, food in a stand, or tickets from a window.
I can make change.

5. *I get along well with people. I make friends easily and enjoy*
*joining clubs and other groups. I am occasionally asked to serve*
*minor offices. I enjoy people and work well with fellow students*
*and adults.* I enjoy selling things and have had considerable success in selling tickets, magazines, etc.

6. *People enjoy working with me and I have good relations with*
*teachers and fellow students. I can speak easily to groups and to*
*individuals. I enjoy working with groups, and positions of lead-*
*ership are often given to me.* I can be quite aggressive without
being objectionable in selling ideas and products.

7. *Convincing people to do what I want them to is an area in*
*which I excel. I am able to win people over to my point of view*
*without antagonizing them. I can usually get what I want without*
*appearing to be aggressive.* I have a knack for working out plans
for promoting products, ideas, or people. I have been elected to
numerous class and/or club offices and am often appointed to
committees. Junior Achievement programs and other free enterprise activities interest me very much. I enjoy and experience considerable success in selling school mementos or other objects in
school fund-raising drives.

## Social Service Field

Study the seven ratings carefully and choose the paragraph
that fits you.

1. *I dislike being bothered with other people's problems. In fact,*
*I don't get mixed up with people if I can help it. I have one or*
*two friends.*

2. *When I try to help my friends out of trouble, I usually end up*
*arguing with them. I seldom tell my troubles to other people, as I*
*think people should work out their problems by themselves. I*
*have a few friends.*

3. *I find it easier to help my friends directly than to help them*
*help themselves. I get along with most of my classmates but I get*
*tired of hearing people talk about their troubles.*

4. *I make friends with most people. I don't always understand*
*why people do what they do, but I try not to get angry with*

*them*. I try to help my friends but I don't go out of my way to be a Good Samaritan.

5. *I get along well with people. My friends often share their difficulties with me and I can usually help them solve their problems.* I take part in student-body functions that are designed to build school spirit and morale.

6. *I am interested in people, and helping them makes me feel good. I usually understand why people act the way they do and accept their actions even though I may not agree with them.* In discussions with my classmates, I am usually able to put myself in their place and understand why they think as they do. I am a member of a school service club, Future Teachers, or American Field Service Club.

7. *People fascinate me. I spend much time in improving the lot of my fellowman. I seem to have the knack of building people's confidence in themselves.* My school activities include tutoring and positions of leadership in service clubs, Future Teachers, and/or American Field Service. I contribute to my community by participation in such volunteer activities as hospital volunteer, boys' club worker, nursery school helper, or church school worker. Activities on the national scene like Peace Corps and Vista appeal to me.

## Verbal Field

Study the seven ratings carefully and choose the paragraph that fits you.

1. *Although it is not hard for me to talk with my friends, I cannot make a report to a group. I can write a simple sentence.* When reading a comic book, I depend a lot on the pictures.

2. *I can write some but not well enough to express ideas. I can write a short letter. I can read simple directions but cannot understand newspaper articles.* When I am talking to people, I can understand what they say as long as they do not use big words. I can learn more by watching television than from reading the newspaper.

3. *Speaking to groups of ten to fifteen people is difficult for me, but I can do so if the topic is familiar to me. I can talk on an informal basis in class.* I can understand what my teachers say without asking a great number of questions. I can read the daily newspaper but have trouble reading some of my school books. It is possible for me to write short compositions and to make written reports on what I have seen or read.

4. *My vocabulary is such that I can usually make myself understood. It is possible for me to make oral reports in class and I feel comfortable doing so. I am able to make good, readable reports but need considerable time to organize my material.* I can read well enough to understand my textbooks. I know how to use a library to find reference books and articles. I can understand teachers' lectures and am able to take part in class discussions that follow teachers' lectures or student reports.

5. *I write and/or speak with ease and read well and with enjoyment. I am able to discuss ideas presented in novels or books or talks made in class. It is possible for me to tell when words are improperly used or when sentences are improperly constructed.* Although my compositions are not very creative, my grammar is good, and my English teacher does not have to put many corrections on my papers. I can make an accurate report on events or scenes I have witnessed or read about. I work as a reporter for the school newspaper.

6. *I read rapidly and have good comprehension. I am able to do research with source books and to write excellent reports. Most of my compositions are returned with few corrections and with numerous positive comments.* When someone else makes a report or speech, I am able to analyze the talk and to make both critical and constructive comments. I speak well enough to express my ideas well and, with coaching, can impart the author's message in recitations and plays. I write feature or interpretive articles for the school paper.

7. *I am an excellent reader. It is not uncommon for me to read an assigned novel the night after it has been assigned. My vocabulary is large and I use it well both in speaking and in writing. I have a flair for writing and as a result my essays and compositions are interesting as well as informative.* I have been successful in writing poems, plays, short stories, and essays. It is possible for me to write and to give a speech that is interesting, informative, and, if need be, persuasive. When I have time I attend debates, plays, speeches, readings, or trials. I contribute to the school literary magazines and/or write editorials for the school paper.

### The Arts Field

This field differs from the other seven in that you are to consider only one of several possible aspects of the field. It is highly unlikely that any one person is proficient at more than one or two of the arts. Therefore, consider only the comments that refer to the art form in which you excel, be it painting, dancing, vocal music, or instrumental music. Study the seven ratings carefully and choose the paragraph that fits you.

1. I attempt to dance but often have trouble. I can trace from other drawings and make stick men. I am able to sing although I cannot really carry a tune. I do not play a musical instrument.

2. I am able to make simple mechanical and straight-line drawings. I dance to slow music. I can carry a tune or am able to pick out a tune on an instrument.

3. I appreciate popular music, tap and popular dancing, or cartoons. I perform at a modest level but not well enough to exhibit my art or perform alone except for comic effect.

4. I dance to most musical rhythms. I can make presentable signs and draw acceptable mechanical drawings. I can carry a tune and can sing in harmony if necessary. I play an instrument for my own satisfaction.

5. My artistic ability is good. I sing in the school chorus, play in the school band or orchestra, dance in the chorus, or draw well enough to have my work displayed around school occasionally. My performance is more mechanical than interpretive, however. I can understand and appreciate classical music, ballet dancing, or modern art.

6. I am able to produce still-life drawings with warmth and feeling. I have soloed or exhibited in school and community functions and have received recognition in the form of high ratings or prizes for my performances. I take private lessons and spend much time in practice.

7. I have unusual talent in art. My performances are interpretive and not mechanical reproductions. I have produced original and creative works; I am able to give expression to my feelings in my art form (music, dance, or art). I go to art museums, concert halls, or dance studios to learn what is new in interpretation and technique. I do not begrudge the hours I spend in practice and lessons. I have held recitals or exhibited in one-man shows.

### Academic Level

Study the seven ratings carefully, choose the paragraph that fits you.

1. *I have trouble reading and find school hard. I learn best if someone shows me what I have to do and tells me how to do it.* The subjects that I can do best are those that require little reading or math.

2. *I can learn from a book by reading the material several times and memorizing the important parts.* I can write a short letter or note and can work arithmetic problems with whole numbers (10 x 15 = 150). However, I learn *best* by being shown and told.

3. *Subjects like math and science are very hard for me. Much of my learning is by listening and observation.* I can learn facts and can read historical and literary passages that describe or tell a story. I need a great deal of help from my teachers to do average work.

4. *If I am to do above-average work I must do much homework and get a great deal of help from my teachers.* I learn best from class discussions, films, and teachers' lectures. I am successful with ordinary explanatory and descriptive writings. I find theoretical concepts difficult to understand and learn.

5. *Although I do not find them easy, I can successfully carry courses like biology, algebra, geometry, or French. I read well and usually read several books a year for pleasure.* I need help from my teachers occasionally. With help, I can perform work that requires reasoning and the application of concepts and principles. If I work moderately hard, I can perform at an above-average level.

6. *It is my general practice to do more than is required of me in readings, experiments, research projects, etc. I write and speak with clarity, force, and originality.* I can interpret and appreciate poetry and good music. My math and reading skills and reasoning ability are such that it is relatively easy for me to do good schoolwork.

7. *Solving abstract problems, performing unusual experiments, doing original research, or doing creative work in the fine arts gives me true satisfaction. When time permits, I do much reading on my own.* I require help from my teachers only for suggestions for advanced and supplementary work. I often solve a problem just because it exists, much like the mountain climber climbs a mountain because it is there. Ideas, words, and number symbols interest me much more than things.

## Motivation Level

Study the seven ratings carefully, choose the paragraph that fits you, and record the rating on the Motivation scale.

1. *I am satisfied with what I know now. I find it hard to work for any type of advancement.* Even with much help, I make little effort to try to achieve. In fact, schoolwork is not important to me.

2. *I try some to succeed in simple school tasks. Only with a great deal of encouragement will I work on hard problems.* It is difficult for me to get interested in any task that I do not think is important.

3. *Much urging by my teachers or parents is necessary to get me to work hard. I will overcome minor obstacles by myself.* It is difficult for me to work on a project or an assignment where results are not seen immediately.

4. *I need some encouragement if I am to overcome serious obstacles. I will achieve on a moderate level on my own.* I will work to capacity only if I can see some evidence of success.

5. *I will stay with difficult tasks if inspired by my teachers. Difficult assignments are, on occasion, completed through my own motivation.* I can work to achieve goals that are two months to a semester away but cannot concentrate on projects that will benefit me one to two years from now.

6. *I overcome arduous tasks through my own motivation. I seldom need urging by my teachers in working to capacity. I usually work beyond the requirements of instructors.* I often do tasks that are unpleasant and difficult just because they are requirements for success in some phase of schoolwork.

7. *I set extremely difficult goals for myself and stick to them until they are attained. I require no supervision from my teachers. It is possible for me to work for goals that are far removed in terms of time.* I push myself harder than do my parents or my teachers. In fact, I've been accused by parents, counselors, or teachers of working too hard. What I may do in the future pulls me constantly and strongly.

## Organization Level

Study the seven ratings carefully and choose the paragraph that fits you.

1. *I have the habit of starting many tasks but finishing few. (Pleasant duties are always done first and less interesting tasks or unliked jobs are put off or not completed.)* My chances of success are best if I study in the classroom and have the help of the teacher.

2. *I seldom complete work assignments made a couple of days in advance. Short-range jobs, however, I usually finish on time.* I am easily sidetracked and have poor powers of concentration.

3. *I need help in organizing or making plans for jobs that require more than one step or stage. Assignments made one day and due the next are usually completed.* Assignments made a week in advance cause trouble, however. They are either not completed or are completed with frantic last-minute activity.

4. *Some of my schoolwork is planned. More often than not, I set up a schedule and stick with it.* Once in a while, however, I let my assignments slip so that by examination time I must spend much time reviewing and learning what should have been covered on schedule.

5. *I usually organize my schoolwork quite well. I seldom put things off and can usually determine the priority that should be given to different tasks.* Only a small portion of the day is wasted. I seldom work ahead of schedule, however, and sometimes I work up to the last minute to complete an assignment on time.

6. *I try to organize my work so there is a small loss of time and effort. Long assignments are scheduled so that library books and research materials are used when they are still available and the findings can be worked into the report or paper properly.* I am not easily disturbed. My work pattern is such that experiments, problems, or projects that contain multiple parts are carried out in proper sequence. In all my activities, first things come first.

7. *I know when and how I study best and have my time organized for maximum performance. I set up a schedule for each task that enables me to finish each assignment in time to permit review and revisions. I have excellent concentration and waste very little time. Cramming for exams is a practice I rarely employ.* Term papers are planned so that I can work in an orderly manner and libraries and other research sources can be maximally used. I know pretty well what I will do with my time for the next year.

## Energy Output Level

Study the seven ratings carefully, choose the paragraph that fits you, and record your rating on the profile.

1. *I tire very easily. I have trouble getting started in the morning and the whole day is usually a drag.* My lack of pep is a serious problem for me. I miss a great deal of school because of illness.

2. *School wears me out. By the time my afternoon classes are held I am beat and can't get much out of them.* Every time a siege of illness hits the school, I get sick. I am usually too tired to study at night.

3. *If I don't take in extra activities, I have enough strength and pep to do my schoolwork. I have serious difficulty doing satisfactory work in my afternoon classes.* Hot weather affects me more than it does most people.

4. *I seem to have as much energy as most of my classmates. I can carry an average or extra class load without becoming tired.* If I overdo for a period of days, however, I become tired and may come down with a cold or need to go to bed for a rest. My attendance record is good.

5. *I can work steadily all day and still have plenty of pep left for evening activities. If I have had a strenuous day, a short rest or nap will snap me back.* I have an occasional cold, but can usually fight it off. I can perform successfully in late afternoon classes, but I tire and my marks suffer.

6. *I seldom find it necessary to take a rest but find that a change of pace, like a short period of relaxation at the end of the school day, is helpful and refreshing. I am able to put in a hard day at school and still have sufficient energy for my studies or other activities at night.* This is true even if I participate in extracurricular activities. I sleep well at night and wake up in the morning ready to go.

7. *It seems I have an unlimited supply of energy. Sicknesses and colds appear to be things that other people get. It is possible for me to do satisfactory work in academic courses meeting in late afternoon periods. This is true even for classes I do not particularly like.* I can work for extended periods on mentally exhausting work without making errors even if I get only short periods of relaxation. I can be bored but seldom tired or fatigued.

# Interests

The eight field scales you completed before the four level scales dealt with your *abilities* in various fields. On this page you will find directions for rating your *interests* in the same eight fields. Read the brief description for the Scientific Field listed below. In this description and those that follow, the nature of the work performed in the field is outlined. The examples list activities related to the field that you may have performed.

1. *Scientific*—The Scientific Field requires curiosity about new products, processes, and ideas. Experimentation and the solution of problems are important aspects of work in this field. Examples: conduct laboratory experiments, read scientific books, make and record exact observations or measurements, collect rocks or bugs or plants.

Choose from the following scale the rating that describes your interest in the Scientific Field.

| 1 | 2 | 3 | 4 | 5 |
|---|---|---|---|---|
| I dislike participating in this field. | I have little interest in this field. | I can take this field or leave it. I am indifferent. | I am interested in this field. | I am very interested in this field. |

Next to the paragraph write the number that best describes your degree of interest. Now do this for each of the other fields; you will find their descriptions below.

2. *Mechanical*—The person working in the Mechanical Field deals with things. He may devise new products. He may use machines to produce things or he may repair machines or equipment. Examples: build a model, sew a garment, repair a machine or appliance, design and build a piece of furniture.

3. *Clerical*—The Clerical Field deals with the communications aspect of business. Producing, reproducing, and filing reports and correspondence are important aspects of this field. Examples: type a letter, proofread an article, file correspondence, take notes, serve as an organization secretary.

4. *Computational*—Working with numbers is the major operation in the Computational Field. This may involve keeping records, solving arithmetic problems, and/or applying mathematical formulas. Examples: compute percentages, work problems, make graphs, solve mathematical puzzles.

5. *Sales*—Selling ideas or products is the most important activity in the Sales Field. This involves working with people for personal profit or gain. Examples: sell tickets or magazines or candy, run for office, persuade others to vote for your candidate or ideas.

6. *Social Service*—Those engaged in the Social Service Field work with people. Their chief aim is to help those with whom they work. Examples: help others with problems, be a good listener, tutor, organize or direct or help with recreational activities.

7. *Verbal*—The Verbal Field is made up of people who work with words. This includes reading, speaking, and writing words. Examples: give speeches, write stories, read a book or article and write a report on it, debate, write for a newspaper.

8. *The Arts*—The Arts Field includes the activities of music, dancing, and art. These may be original, creative works or performances of the works of others. Concern yourself only with the form of art you like most. Examples: play an instrument, make a painting, sing solo or in a group, dance solo or in a chorus, make a sculpture or clay figure.

As before, discuss your responses with each other.

## Activity Seven

### *What Is Important to Me?*

Place a number 1 before the item that is most important to you, number 2 next to the one that is next in importance, and so forth.

1. satisfying and successful career
2. job security
3. good family relationships
4. a world without discrimination
5. international fame
6. pleasure
7. strong religious faith
8. lovely home in a beautiful setting
9. self-knowledge
10. ability or position to influence world affairs
11. satisfying love relationship
12. the right to do what I want
13. excitement
14. ability to stimulate and/or influencce the minds of others
15. enough money to be comfortable

16. sense of accomplishment
17. a world in which man and nature are in balance
18. love and understanding of friends

Discuss your ranking as a family, asking these questions, "What have I learned about myself? How might it influence my life? my career?

## Activity Eight

### What about the World
### Makes Me Mad and What in the World Needs Doing? [5]

This activity is one that will stretch over time, but you can begin it now and add to it later. As a family, brainstorm these two questions. This may give you an idea of a career that could give you satisfaction, since it would give you a feeling of accomplishment. Make a list to put in your folder and keep adding to it as you think of things. You may get an idea as you read the newspapers and watch television.

### Putting it Together

In this chapter you and your children have had an opportunity to look at your interests, aptitudes, and values. For a culminating activity, you should each write a brief narrative on your ideal life-style. Project yourself five, ten, or fifteen years ahead. Your ideal life-style includes such things as where in the world you would like to live so that you can enjoy your leisure activities as well as your work. Describe the area: large city, country, suburb, or other. Tell about the family you would like, what you would like to do together, and how much time you would like to spend with each other. Ask your children if they want children of their own. Why do they want children? How many do they want? Why do they want that many? You should each describe your ideal house or apartment. Do you want cultural things close at hand? What about other recreational facilities? Describe the things you would like to do in your job. What do you see yourself doing in your leisure time? What kind of people do you want to live near? work with?

The activities you have completed in this chapter should help you answer these questions; if you need to refer back to them, do so. After you have all completed your narratives, read them aloud to each other, leaving out any parts you do not wish to

40

share. Discuss them. Feel free to point out conflicts of values, interests, or aptitudes you see in each other's narratives—for example, "You said you wanted to be able to sail in your leisure time; can you do that on the salary you will make as a waitress?"

Feel free to change any parts you want to. You and your children may have a limited awareness, at this point, of the career options open to you. After you have finished with the book, you will probably want to complete this activity again.

# 2

---

## EXPANDING
## CAREER
## AWARENESS

---

You and your children now have a general idea of the kind of life you would like to lead and some information generated from the interest inventories about possible careers. This is just the beginning. There is more than one career that can satisfy your desired quality of life, but where in the world are these careers and what are they?

You probably have a very limited idea of the wide variety of jobs in existence. Just for fun, let's find out exactly how extensive your career awareness is. Take three minutes right now to write down as many job titles as you can possibly think of.

If you listed thirty, you are about average. There are 50,000 job titles presently listed in the Dictionary of Occupational Titles published by the Department of Labor. New job titles are added every two years, and others are deleted; the list does not remain static.

Your children must not only learn skills to assess how they have changed, but they must also develop skills to find information about what is available on the job market. Before they can utilize these skills, however, they must expand their career awareness. With a little effort you can take some of the activities you all do for pleasure and make career awareness activities of them. Let us look at a few possibilities.

## For Young Children

### *Watching Television*

Many television shows have careers depicted in them; they are not always accurate, but contain at least some information. For example, *The Mary Tyler Moore Show* illustrates the careers of newspaper reporter, editor, news reporting anchor man, and script writer. *Hawaii Five-O*, *The Streets of San Francisco*, *Colombo*, *Mannix*, *Cannon*, and *Barnaby Jones* all depict people working in the police department. *Emergency* shows paramedics at work. With younger children, you can simply ask them after the program, "From what you see on this program, what do you think police people do? Would you like to work for the police? Do you think this program shows you the real things police people do?"

The next step to be carried out is to see real police people at work. It quickly beomes obvious that the shows are dramatized and that the roles, at least in some cases, are stereotyped. Children may learn at this point that they cannot necessarily tell from television shows and movies what a person does.

In the case of older children (ages twelve to seventeen), you can ask them to write a job description of the person on the show. A job description consists of major job responsibilities, minor job responsibilities, skills necessary for employment, personal qualities recommended for the work, kind of training necessary, salary range, advantages, and disadvantages. It is a good idea to build in the concept of life-style by having them see if they can find clues to leisure time activities, family life, and so on. (For example, Cannon likes to eat.) They should definitely follow up this investigation with an interview of someone engaged in this career to check for stereotypes.

### *Visiting Cultural Events*
### *(Museums, Art Galleries,*
### *Theatrical Productions)*

Parents can get permission to bring their children behind the scenes to see people who work to make cultural events a reality. One family went backstage after a matinee performance of *Tosca* at the San Francisco Opera and talked to people working as stage hands, costume designers, hairdressers, makeup artists, musicians, actors, lighting technicians, sound technicians, and photographers. They were willing to tell the family briefly about what they did, how they liked their jobs, and how they lived their lives.

### Having Family Portraits Taken

Take time during a portrait sitting to have the children find out how the photographer got her or his job. Ask what made her decide to be a photographer, or what he liked as a child that led him to this career.

### Reading Books

After reading a fictional book, ask the question, "What careers were depicted in this novel and why did the author use these careers to put across the story?"

### Taking an Automobile Trip

To keep children from becoming bored while on a journey, have them name all the careers they can think of that made the trip possible. Some examples are auto line workers, service station attendants, auto mechanics, road service people, motel workers, and waitresses. Or the children could name every job of which they see any representation on the trip—for example, truck drivers, telephone line workers, telephone operators, electricians, architects, and construction workers. This activity can be applied to almost any form of travel.

### Dining

Name all the careers that make it possible to have dinner out. Examples are farmers, agriculture specialists, truck drivers, farm workers, cooks, waitresses, agriculture equipment salesmen, and fertilizer manufacturers. This same activity can be performed while shopping, visiting a hospital, or taking advantage of some other service. The point of these exercises is not necessarily to force choices, but to expand the awareness of careers. Children and young adults generally have a very limited awareness of the many careers available to them.

### Comic Strips

Together, pick out and discuss careers or career concepts from the comic strips. You should also keep in mind or write down the stereotypes depicted. For instance, *Brenda Starr* is a career reporter, and the stereotype is of a glamorous person. In *Dick*

*Tracy* the career is that of a policeman, and the stereotype is one of sternness. In *Beetle Bailey,* a military person is depicted, and the stereotype is of a goof-off. Some good discussion questions are: Do we sometimes base decisions on stereotypes? Do we know people in these careers who contradict the stereotypes?

## Charades

Each family member chooses a career to act out and the rest try to guess what it is.

## Twenty Questions

A good activity for a trip or even at home is "Twenty Questions." One person thinks of a career and the others ask questions that can be answered yes or no in order to determine what it is. If other members cannot guess after asking twenty questions, the one who is "it" tells the answer and gets another turn.

## Hats

Little children love to wear hats. At a second-hand store, buy hats that people wear on their jobs for your children to use when they play. Some examples follow: policeman's hat, construction worker's hard hat, nurse's cap, fireman's hat, football helmet, army cap, sailor's hat, and chef's hat. Or children can make their own hats from a picture by coloring, folding, and pasting paper.

## Maps

Put a map of your town on the wall and give the children a map to bring with them when you do your errands. Have them follow your route. They can locate places of business on the map as they pass them. When you return home, they can paste a piece of paper on the map with the names on it of the businesses visited. Ask them, "What do you think people do who work there?" In addition to expanding awareness of careers, this also assists in map reading, spelling, and reading.

## Fantasies

Small children have fantasies about what they would like to be. Explore with them their fantasies. Be careful not to place your values on them or to sex-stereotype careers. If your daughter wants to be a carpenter, encourage her to find out what a carpenter does. This is also a clue to buying toys; a small tool chest for Christmas would fit such a case well.

### Field Trips
### (Sounds and Sights of
### the Work World)

If there is some construction going on in your community, why not take the long way home from your errands and drop by? You can say, "Pay close attention, and when we get home I'd like to have you draw a picture of what you see and hear." Put these pictures up for older family members to see and let the children describe their trip and picture.

The same thing can be done for your trip to the cleaners, grocery store, bank, auto shop, department store, and so forth.

### Dodge Ball

Here is a good activity for a birthday party. Two children act as salespersons, and the rest of the children as buyers. Each child holds several pieces of candy. Salespersons take turns throwing the ball and trying to "sell" one of the customers by hitting him or her with the ball. When a buyer is hit, he or she gives a candy to the salesperson. As the children lose all their candy, they are eliminated from the game. The last two customers to get out become the salespeople for the next round.

### Going to the Zoo

On a trip to the zoo, have children consider what jobs are necessary to keep the animals cared for. Children usually love animals. After this you could visit a pet shop (though you may end up buying one of the animals), a veterinarian, the humane society, the dog pound, a game warden, a race track, a pet-grooming establishment and so on, and discover all the people who work in animal care.

### Cutting Up Magazines

On a rainy afternoon you can give children old magazines and have them cut out pictures of people engaged in different work and play activities. Have them put the ones they think would be fun in one pile and those they do not think they would like in another. Afterwards, if you have time, ask them why they dislike or like them. With your help they can also try to identify what the workers are doing and where they work.

### *Family Discussions*

It is important for children to talk about other aspects of work, such as relationships between careers and relationships between leisure and work. Following are some concepts, along with sample questions, useful in getting a discussion going with young children, perhaps around the dinner table.

## 1. People have different interests, abilities, and attitudes.

a. How are we different from one another?
b. How are we like one another?
c. How are Mom and Dad different from the parents of your friends?
d. How are you different from your friends?
e. Is it good to be different?
f. Is it important to be different?
g. How can being different affect the work you do when you grow up?
h. What would happen in the world if all people were alike?
i. What are some kinds of work you think _____ (member of the family) would like to do?

## 2. People change, and we should accept the fact that we will all be different a few years from now.

a. Do you like to do exactly the same things you did last year or two years ago?
b. How are you different?
c. Have Mom and Dad changed?
d. Have your brothers and sisters changed? How?
e. Have your friends changed?
f. What do you think you will be like in two years?
g. Do adults change?
h. Can you think of certain ways in which adults you know have changed?
i. Do you think the ways in which you change will affect how you will feel about your job?
j. What can you do about it?

### 3. Your skills and abilities in certain school subjects and playtime activities can be a clue to what careers you would have success in and enjoy.

a. What subjects in school do you enjoy?
b. What subjects in school do you do the best in?
c. What kinds of playtime activities are you best in?
d. Can you think of jobs that use any of these subjects or activities?
e. As you look at jobs should you keep these things in mind?

### 4. Some careers require more education than others and some careers allow more leisure and different leisure activities.

a. What people that you know of seem to have more playtime?
b. What do these people do in their work?
c. What people you know seem to have little time for leisure?
d. What do these people do in their jobs?
e. Do you think there are some jobs that allow more leisure time? What are they?
f. Are there some jobs that do not allow much leisure time? What are they?
g. How much time do you want for leisure?
h. Which jobs that you know of require more schooling?
i. Which jobs require little schooling?
j. How much schooling do you think you would like to have?

### 5. There are different ways to train for a job.

a. What are some ways that people can be trained for jobs?
b. Does the amount of schooling affect how much you will make on your job?
c. What kinds of training cost the most? the least?
d. Does more education required for a job mean that the job is more important?
e. Is one kind of training better than another?
f. Does the amount and kind of training necessary to get a job mean that the job will pay more? be more enjoyable?

## 6. One person's work is
## another person's play.

a. What kind of leisure activities can you think of that some people do in their jobs?
b. Do you think some people enjoy doing things for play that other people consider work?
c. In our family, do some family members' leisure activities seem like work to you?

## 7. Enjoying work depends on how
## you get along with your co-workers.

a. Are there some people you enjoy working with more than others?
b. What are the traits of people you enjoy working with? of those you do not like working with?
c. As you look at work places, are there some that you think you would like working in because of the people you see working there?
d. Do you see places where you would not like to work because of the people you see working there?

## For Older Children and Young Adults

Some of the activities described for younger children can be adapted for older children, because young people and adults often have a limited awareness of career options also. In addition to modified activities for young children, certain activities especially for young adults can be useful, particulary in developing the information-seeking skills they need.

Information about oneself and about jobs available eventually becomes obsolete—that is, one's aptitudes, interests, and values change, and so does the labor market picture. Therefore, it is important to teach a process through which young people and adults can recycle themselves at any age. As has been stated before, it is not realistic to expect a forty-year-old to live with an eighteen-year-old's decisions.

In chapter one you were provided with activities to assist in assessing yourself. This chapter is designed to give you and your children skills for assessing the world of work. Once your children understand the process, they can use it again and again, at age sixteen, twenty, thirty-one, forty-five, or sixty. One thing is important for them to understand: *they* are in control. Unfortunately, many people do not believe this.

## Interviewing

Your neighborhood is an excellent resource for career information. Young people are at first reluctant to interview neighbors about their life-style, so the best way to start is to have your children interview you.

There are two types of interviews that can be helpful: one stresses the worker in the career development process, and the other stresses the job. Both perspectives are important, and neighbors, relatives, and friends are a source of both. Once young people feel comfortable in the interview, they should do it as often as possible. They may use tape recorders for playback, or they may take notes.

### The Job Interview

Using the following list of questions as a base, let them begin by interviewing you. Other questions can be added.

1. What special interests or skills do you need for your job?
2. For what other occupations are you qualified with your knowledge and training?
3. In what ways can I get this job—through training, college, or experience?
4. What type of person do you have to be in order to like and be successful at your job?
5. What are all the different jobs you have had and which have led to the one you have now?
6. Do you think that your mistakes have helped you to make better decisions?
7. What types of interests do you have and how did they help you decide what job you wanted?
8. What school subjects do you use in your work and how?
9. How has your particular job changed over the past ten or twenty years? What do you think it will be like in another ten years?
10. How does this job support your way of living in terms of income, knowledge, working hours, and leisure time?
11. Are your hobbies similar to or different from your job?
12. Why is this job important to you? What satisfaction do you

get? Do you know of any common factors a person should possess to be successful in the world of work?

After your children have conducted such an interview, it is a good idea to have them do a brief analysis. Ideally, this is done in writing and placed in their career folder. The extent to which the interviewing and follow-up is done depends on their motivation, which should come from within them and should not be mandated by you.

This format can be used for a written job analysis:

Job title
General job description (3 or 4 sentences is enough)
Skills required in the job
Personal characteristics applicable to success in the job
Advantages of the job
Disadvantages of the job
Salary range
Related careers
Educational and training routes to job entry
Certification, licensing, etc., necessary for job entry, if any
Types of institutions hiring people in these jobs
Personal analysis of interview: the parts of the job I would like or dislike

In all cases, the family should discuss these interviews afterwards. Parents can and should conduct interviews also. Obviously, the commitment of the family to this task will vary greatly, but the greater the commitment, the greater the benefits will be. It can also be very interesting and rewarding.

### Worker Interview

In this case, one should choose a person who has been in the work force at least ten years. One might ask the following questions.

1. What was your earliest childhood fantasy career?
2. Did you have any other career fantasies?
3. What was your first volunteer job? Examples: babysitting brothers and sisters, teaching Sunday school, etc.
4. What did you like and dislike about this job?
5. What were some of your other volunteer jobs, and what did you like and dislike about them?
6. What was your first paid job?
7. What did you like and dislike about this job?

8. What were your significant subsequent jobs to the present, and what did you like and dislike about each?

9. What do you expect to be doing in ten years? Why?

10. What would you like to be doing in ten years? Why?

11. Personal analysis: what factors do you see operating in this person's career history? Examples: changes were made usually for money, the career appears to have security as its basis, the changes were effected by circumstances beyond the control of that person, changes were made to escape boredom.

This biography can also provide a very interesting and worthwhile discussion.

### Reading Newspaper Features, News, and Want Ads

The newspaper is an excellent source of career information and a source for expanding both career awareness and information-seeking skills. The want ads are a logical beginning. You and your children should first circle all the want ads advertising a job that sounds interesting at first glance. After you have each done this, go back and write the names of the other members of the family next to ads you think they would enjoy and do well. You can then share these with each other.

After you have finished with the want ads, scan the rest of the paper for other career information. News and features often give information such as local strikes, appointment of new bank managers, new building projects, new store openings, and so on. See if you can glean any information from the story, and share it with each other.

As was mentioned in the first chapter, career choice affects the geographical setting where one lives, and vice versa. On a trip, buy local newspapers and go through the same procedure. Do you see any differences in available jobs and life-styles of the people in the area? Newspapers accurately depict life-style; The life-style in Albuquerque, for example, is different from the life-style in New York City, and this shows in the newspapers. Discuss and try the local life-style against your values and interests. Does it fit?

When you go on a business trip, bring back a newspaper for the family to look at. The differing sizes of towns, as well as their different geographical locations, affect job availability and life-style and so should be looked at as well. If your family is really committed, you could write to different chambers of commerce to ask for sample newspapers and local information. This can be a source for expanding career options and understanding their changing availability by area.

### The Yellow Pages

Get extra telephone directories for each member of the family from your local telephone company. If you are from a very small town, try to get one from a larger city. Go through the directory thoroughly, and with each classification heading ask yourself the question, "Am I interested in this line of work?" Follow the first reaction that comes to your mind. If your answer is yes or maybe, write down the heading. After you have your list, look at the values you have already identified, as well as your ideal life-style, and see if you can eliminate some careers immediately.

After you have a manageable list, go back through the yellow pages and notice the companies that hire these people; if you really want more good information, get in touch with these companies and see if you can interview someone in that field. Most companies are willing to let you do this.

Older children and young adults often have a limited understanding of the concepts related to career choice, job satisfaction, the relationship between leisure and work, and so forth, and, like young children, can benefit from discussing some of these concepts. Some of the concepts are the same as those for young children, but obviously the questions are different. Sample questions will be given with each concept to help start the discussion off.

### 1. Individuals differ in their interests, aptitudes, abilities, values, and attitudes.

How have we demonstrated as a family that this is true and what implications does this have for choice of careers and life-styles?

### 2. Self-development is a lifelong process and is constantly changing as a result of life experiences.

a.  What experiences have you had that, you feel, have changed your interests, aptitudes, values, or attitudes?

54

b.  Do you expect to change in the future?
c.  How will this change affect your job satisfaction?

### 3. The change in environment
### affects one's career choice.

a.  What changes in the environment could affect the labor market for you (examples: federal legislation, energy sources, getting married)?
b.  How can you find out what the trends are in environmental concerns?
c.  What jobs coming into existence could interest you? Which of your skills might be applicable?

### 4. Individuals must be adaptable
### to a changing society.

a.  What might be your reaction to having your job wiped out?
b.  What can you do to prepare for this?

### 5. Career planning is each
### person's responsibility.

a.  Do you believe this?
b.  What role do parents play?
c.  What should happen if children and parents have a conflict in this area?
d.  How is our family handling this issue?

### 6. Knowledge and skills in
### school subjects are important
### to consider in career planning.

a.  What subjects are you good at?
b.  What careers use these skills?
c.  In what subjects are you doing poorly or lacking interest?
d.  What kinds of careers use these skills?

### 7. The expectations of society
### influence our career choices.

a.  What societal pressures are you influenced by? How? Are there certain careers considered inappropriate by your family? church? friends? school? neighbors?
b.  How do you deal with these pressures?

## 8. There is a relationship between commitment to education and work and the availability and use of leisure time.

a. How much school do you want to attend and why?
b. What jobs will give you the leisure you want to enjoy?
c. How many hours a week do you want to work?

## 9. There are many training routes available to you.

a. What kinds of training routes are available?
b. Which one appeals to you?
c. For your career options which training routes are appropriate?

## 10. Work means different things to different people.

a. What does work mean to you?
b. Can one person's work be another person's leisure? If so, name a few examples.

## 11. Job satisfaction depends, in part, on the kinds of people with whom you work and the physical environment in which you work.

a. With what kind of people do you like to work?
b. With what kind of people do you not like to work?
c. Describe your ideal physical and psychological work environment.

## 12. As one becomes specialized one becomes more dependent on other workers.

a. What careers do you know of that are dependent on workers in other jobs? Example: Doctor—dependent on nurses, technologists, etc.
b. What careers are relatively free of dependence on other workers? Example: real estate salespeople.

## Library Work

When your children visit the library, have them look at sources of career information. Trade magazines, for instance, are excellent sources of information. Most associations have a trade magazine which not only gives you up-to-date information on the issues that face workers in that career but lists advertisements for training schools and job opportunities. Ask your research or reference librarian for these trade magazines; if the supply is limited, ask to see the listing of associations and write to them for a sample copy of their trade magazine and other career information. Also, ask at the library to see *Ulrich's Periodicals Directory* and the *Encyclopedia of Associations* by the Gale Research Company. Write to some of these associations as well. You may be barraged by mail, but it will give you a real feel for the career.

Now you have not only a process for self-evaluation but one for obtaining information from the outside world. The world will change, but the process will not. Your children can go through it at different times throughout their life, and, incidentally, so can you. Remember, *you* are in control. Getting the information is your own responsibility.

# 3

## PERSONALITY
## AND
## SUCCESS

We have discussed how differences in interests, attitudes, and values affect the choice of a life-style and career options within that life-style. But what about those other qualities that differentiate people into personality types? Do these have an effect on career choice or happiness in a given career?

Certainly you realize already the uniqueness of each of your children. You may not be able to put your finger on exactly what makes one different from another, but somehow they seem to approach life in different ways. In a society that appears to value conformity, the uniqueness of individuals is often overlooked. This uniqueness, which goes deeper than aptitudes, interests, and values, should be considered when choosing a life-style and exploring careers that can provide your children with a satisfying life.

The Swiss psychiatrist, Carl Jung, proposed the theory that many differences that appear to occur randomly in human behavior are actually systematic and consistent.[6] You have probably heard people described as engineer types, artist types, accountant types, and so on, but have you really thought about what that means? Not all engineers have the same life-style; yet do they have some characteristics in common? Could it be that the differences evident in these career types are due to certain differences in the way they use perception and judgment?

According to Jung, this is true. Perception includes the processes of becoming aware of things, people, occurrences, and ideas.

Judgment includes the processes of coming to conclusions about what has been perceived. If people differ systematically in what they perceive and in the conclusions they come to, they may, as a result, differ in their reactions, interests, values, needs, and motivations. If your children understand what their personality types are, it can assist them in choosing their career options.

The Myers-Briggs Type Indicator[7] is an instrument that helps people discover their type. Even without taking it you may be able to recognize your type from the following illustrations of the differences between one type and another. Just for fun, get your family together to see if each member can recognize her or his own type and perhaps help you to recognize yours. As in the other exercises, discuss the results afterwards and talk about how this bit of information can help in a career search.

### Introduction to Type,
### by Isabel Briggs-Myers

#### *Opposite Kinds of*
#### *Perception and Judgment*

The Type Indicator is concerned with the valuable differences in people resulting from the way they like to perceive and judge. Succeeding at anything takes both perception and judgment. First one must find out what the problem or situation is and what the various things are that might be done about it. Then one must decide which to do. Finding out is an exercise of perception; deciding is an exercise of judgment. There are two basic ways of finding out and two basic ways of deciding.

#### Opposite ways of finding out:
#### sensing and intuition

One way to find out is through *sensing* (S). Eyes, ears, and other senses tell what is actually there and actually happening. Sensing is especially useful for gathering the facts of a situation. The other way to find out is through *intuition,* (N) which shows meanings and relationships and possibilities beyond the reach of the senses. Intuition is especially useful for seeing what might be done about a situation. A person uses both sensing and intuition, of course, but not both at once and not, in most cases, with equal liking.

One who likes sensing better than intuition makes more use of sensing, gets to be more skillful with it, and grows expert at noticing all the observable facts. Such a person tends to become realistic, practical, observant, fun-loving, and good at remembering a great number of facts and working with them.

One who likes intuition better than sensing makes more use of intuition, gets to be .more skillful with it, and grows expert at seeing a new possibility or solution. This person tends to value imagination and inspirations and to become good at forming new ideas and projects and at problem solving.

## Opposite ways of deciding: thinking and feeling

One way to decide is through *thinking* (T). Thinking predicts the logical result of any particular action taken. Then it decides impersonally, on the basis of cause and effect. The other way to decide is through *feeling* (F). Feeling takes into account anything that matters or is important to the person or to others, without requiring that it be logical, and decides on the basis of personal values. A person uses both thinking and feeling, of course, but not both at once and not, in most cases, with equal confidence.

One who trusts thinking more than feeling and uses it more grows to be most skillful in dealing with that part of the world which behaves logically, like machinery, with no unpredictable human reactions. That person tends to become logical, objective, and consistent and to make decisions by analyzing and weighing the facts, including the unpleasant ones.

One who trusts and uses feeling more than thinking grows most skillful in dealing with people. This person tends to become sympathetic, appreciative, and tactful and to give great weight, when making any decisions, to the personal values that are involved, including those of other people.

The kind of perception one prefers to use, either sensing or intuition, can team up with whichever kind of judgment one prefers to use, either thinking or feeling. So there are four possible combinations, each producing a different set of characteristics— different interests, different values, different needs, different habits of mind, and different surface traits.

Each individual's own combination of perception and judgment makes a lot of difference in the kind of work he or she will do best and enjoy. If a man's daily work most needs the kind of perception he naturally prefers, he will handle the job better and find it more satisfying. If a woman's daily work most needs the kind of deciding that comes naturally to her, her decisions will be better and will be made with more confidence. It is important, then, in choosing among careers, to find out how much chance each will offer your child to use his or her own combination of perception and judgment.

### Effects of the Combinations
### of Perception and Judgment

#### Sensing plus Thinking

ST people are mainly interested in facts, since facts are what can be collected and verified directly by the senses—seeing, hearing, touching, and so forth. They make decisions on these facts by impersonal analysis, because the kind of judgment they trust is thinking, with its step-by-step process of reasoning from cause to effect, from premise to conclusion.

#### Sensing plus Feeling

SF people are also interested in facts, but make their decisions with personal warmth because the kind of judgment they trust is feeling, with its power to weigh how much things matter to themselves and to others.

#### Intuition plus Feeling

NF people make decisions with the same personal warmth. But, since they prefer intuition, their interest is not in facts but in possibilities—new projects, things that have not happened yet but might be made to happen, new truths that are not yet known but might be found out, or, above all, new possibilities for people.

#### Intuition plus Thinking

NT people share the interest in possibilities but, since they prefer thinking, they approach these possibilities with impersonal analysis. Often the possibility they choose is a theoretical or technical one, more or less ignoring the human element.

By identifying the column that comes closest to describing her or him, one can tell which two of the four processes (sensing, intuition, thinking, and feeling) she or he naturally uses most. One of those two will be the "favorite" process; the other is the "auxiliary," which supplies perception if the favorite is a judging process ($T$ or $F$), or judgment if the favorite is a perceptive process ($S$ or $N$). A person's

|  | ST<br>Sensing & Thinking | SF<br>Sensing & Feeling | NF<br>Intuition & Feeling | NT<br>Intuition & Thinking |
|---|---|---|---|---|
| People who prefer: |  |  |  |  |
| focus their attention on: | facts | facts | possibilities | possibilities |
| and handle these with: | impersonal analysis | personal warmth | personal warmth | impersonal analysis |
| Thus they tend to become: | practical and matter-of-fact | sympathetic and friendly | enthusiastic and insightful | logical and ingenious |
| and find scope for their abilities in: | technical skills with facts and objects | practical help and services for people | understanding and communicating with people | theoretical and technical developments |
| for example: | applied science, business, production, construction, etc. | patient care, community service sales, teaching, etc. | behavioral science, research, literature and art, teaching, etc. | physical science, research, management, forecasts and analysis, etc. |

greatest strengths come from the two preferred processes, and it is important to trust and develop them. However, for some purposes, the less-liked kinds of perception and judgment will serve much better—if one remembers and takes the trouble to use them.

### Making Full Use of
### Perception and Judgment

To make full use of perception and judgment one needs to use both kinds of perception and both kinds of judgment, each for the right purpose. This is a skill acquired by practice. To solve any problem, make any decision, or deal with any situation, one should exercise each process by itself, consciously and purposefully, so that each can make its own contribution to the solution without interference from any other process. It is best to start with the perceptive processes (S and N), since perception should always come before judgment.

**1. Sensing** is used for facing the facts, being realistic, finding exactly what the situation is and what all people involved are doing. All wishful thinking or sentiment that may blind one to the realities must be put aside and the situation considered as if by a wise, impartial bystander.

**2. Intuition** is used to discover all the possibilities—all the ways in which the situation, its handling, or other people's attitudes toward it might be changed. The natural assumption that one has been doing the one and only obviously right thing must be put aside.

**3. Thinking judgment** is used in an impersonal analysis of cause and effect, including all the consequences of the alternative solutions, both pleasant and unpleasant, both those that weigh against the preferred solution and those in its favor. One must try to count the full cost of everything and examine every misgiving suppressed out of loyalty to someone, liking for something, or reluctance to change.

**4. Feeling judgment** is used to weigh just how deeply one cares about the things that will be gained or lost by each of the alternative solutions. It enables one to make a fresh appraisal, trying not to let the temporary outweigh the permanent, however agreeable or disagreeable the immediate prospect may be. It also prompts one to consider how the other people concerned will feel about the various outcomes, whether their reactions seem reasonable or not. All feelings of all people involved should be included along with the other facts in deciding which solution will work out best.

A person following this process will probably choose, as usual, a solution that appeals to his or her favorite process, but on a sounder basis than usual because the decision will consider facts, possibilities, consequences, and human values. Ignoring any of these can lead to trouble. For instance, intuitives may base a decision on some possibility without discovering the facts that will make it impossible, while sensing types may settle for a faulty solution to a problem because they assume no better one is possible. Thinking types may ignore human values, and feeling types may ignore consequences.

Each person will find some steps in this exercise easier than others. The steps that use an individual's best processes are rather fun. The others are harder, but worthwhile. If feeling is the favorite process, the attempt to see *all* the consequences of an act may reveal that even the best intentions can go wrong unless thought through. If thinking is the preferred process, the attempt to learn how others feel about one's plans may uncover the reasons for their opposition.

What makes certain steps so difficult is the fact that they call for strengths of types other than one's own. When the problem is important, it may be wise to consult someone to whom these strengths come naturally. It is startling to see how different a given situation can look to a person of opposite type, but it can enable one to understand and use the neglected opposite side better.

## Mutual Usefulness of Opposite Types

The clearest vision of the future comes only from an intuitive, the most practical realism only from a sensing type, the most incisive analysis only from a thinker, and the most skillful handling of people only from a feeling type. The success of any enterprise demands a variety of types, each in the right place.

Opposite types can supplement each other in any joint undertaking. When two people approach a problem from opposite sides, each sees things not visible to the other. Unfortunately, they seldom see each other's point of view, so that too much oppositeness makes it hard for people to work well together. The best teamwork is usually done by people who differ on one or two preferences only. This much difference is useful, and the two or three preferences they have in common help them to understand each other and communicate.

When extreme opposites must work or live together, an understanding of type does much to lessen the friction. Disagreement is less irritating when Smith recognizes that it would hardly be normal for Jones to agree. Jones is not being willfully contrary—he is simply an opposite type, and opposite types can be tremendously useful when given the chance. The lists below show some of the specific ways.

---

### Intuitive Needs a Sensing Type—

- to bring up pertinent facts.
- to apply experience to problems.
- to read the fine print in a contract.
- to notice what needs attention now.
- to have patience.
- to keep track of essential details.
- to face difficulties with realism.
- to remind that the joys of the present are important.

### Sensing Type Needs an Intuitive—

- to bring up new possibilities.
- to supply ingenuity on problems.
- to read the signs of coming change.
- to see how to prepare for the future.
- to have enthusiasm.
- to watch for new essentials.
- to tackle difficulties with zest.
- to show that the joys of the future are worth working for.

---

### Feeling Type Needs a Thinker—

- to analyze.
- to organize.
- to find the flaws in advance.
- to reform what needs reforming.
- to hold consistently to a policy.

### Thinker Needs a Feeling Type—

- to persuade.
- to conciliate.
- to forecast how others will feel.
- to arouse enthusiasm.
- to teach.
- to sell.

66

- to weigh "the law and the evidence."
- to fire people when necessary.
- to stand firm against opposition.

- to advertise.
- to appreciate the thinker.

---

## *Remaining Preferences and Summary*

### Outer world or inner world
### ( *E* or *I*)

An individual's main fields of interest are apt to be directly related to the kind of perception and kind of judgment she or he prefers, that is, to the *SN* and *TF* preferences. But the sort of work she or he will most enjoy doing within those fields may depend on the *EI* preference—use of the favorite process extrovertedly (*E*), in the outer world of people and things, or introvertedly (*I*), in the inner world of concepts and ideas.

Take the *ST* people, for example. The introverts among them (*IST*) like to organize facts and principles related to a situation, which is the useful thing to do in economics or law. The extroverts among them (*EST*) like to organize the situation itself (including any idle bystanders) and get it moving, which is the useful thing to do in business or industry.

Jung, who invented the terms, looked upon extroversion and introversion as valuable opposites everyone uses, though not with equal ease. Extroverts tend to be more interested and comfortable when they are working actively with people or things. Introverts tend to be more interested and comfortable when their work involves ideas and requires a good deal of their activity to take place quietly inside their heads.

### Judging attitude or perceptive
### attitude toward the
### outer world (*J* or *P*)

The final preference, *JP*, is between the use of perception and the use of judgment in dealing with the outer world. The *J* people rely mainly on a judging process for this purpose (thinking or feeling, whichever they prefer), and live in a planned, decided, orderly way, wanting to regulate life and control it. The *P* people rely mainly on a perceptive process (sensing or intuition) for dealing with the outer world, and live in a flexible, spontaneous way, wanting to understand life and adapt to it.

This *JP* preference is decided differently for extroverts and introverts. With extroverts the favorite process is, by definition, the one they prefer to use in the outer world. Therefore the extroverts' favorite process governs their *JP* preference. Extroverts whose *favorite process* is a judging one come out *J*, while extroverts whose favorite process is a perceptive one come out *P*.

With introverts the favorite process is, by definition, the one they prefer to use in the inner world. They do their extroverting mostly with their auxiliary. Their *auxiliary process,* therefore, is what governs their *JP* preference. Introverts whose favorite process is a judging one come out *P*, because their auxiliary is perceptive, and introverts whose favorite process is a perceptive one come out *J*.

### Summary of the four preferences.

A person's type is the result of her or his own combination of preferences, stated for convenience in four letters. For example, *ISTJ* means an introvert liking sensing and thinking and a mainly judging attitude toward the outer world. *ENFP* means an extrovert liking intuition and feeling and a mainly perceptive attitude toward the outer world. (*N* is used for intuition because *I* stands for introversion.)

EI *Preference*
Extroversion          Introversion

SN *Preference*
Sensing          Intuition

TF *Preference*
Thinking          Feeling

JP *Preference*
Judgment          Perception

## Effects of Each Preference
## in Work Situations

---

### Introverts—

- like quiet for concentration.
- tend to be careful with details and dislike sweeping statements.
- have trouble remembering names and faces.
- tend not to mind working on one project for a long time uninterruptedly.
- are interested in the idea behind their job.
- dislike telephone intrusions and interruptions.
- like to think carefully before they act, if they act.
- work contentedly alone.
- have some problems communicating.

### Extroverts—

- like variety and action
- tend to be faster and dislike complicated procedures.
- are often good at greeting people.
- are often impatient with long, slow jobs.
- are interested in the results of their job, in getting it done, and in how other people do it.
- often don't mind the interruption of answering the telephone.
- often act quickly, sometimes without thinking.
- like to have other people around.
- usually communicate well.

---

### Feeling Types—

- tend to be very aware of other people and their feelings.
- enjoy pleasing people even in unimportant things.
- like harmony. Their efficiency may be badly disturbed by office feuds.
- often let their decisions be influenced by their own or other people's personal likes and wishes.
- need occasional praise.
- dislike telling people unpleasant things.

### Thinking Types—

- are relatively unemotional and uninterested in people's feelings.
- may hurt people's feelings without knowing it.
- like analyzing and putting things into logical order. They can get along without harmony.
- tend to decide impersonally, sometimes ignoring people's wishes.
- need to be treated fairly.
- are able to reprimand people or fire them when necessary.

69

## Effects of Each Preference in Work Situations (Continued)

- relate well to most people.
- tend to be sympathetic.

- tend to relate well only to other thinking types.
- may seem hard-hearted.

---

### Intuitive Types—

- like solving new problems.
- dislike doing the same thing over and over again.
- enjoy learning a new skill more than using it.
- work in bursts of energy powered by enthusiasm, with slack periods in between.
- put two and two together quickly.
- are patient with complicated situations.
- are impatient with routine details.
- follow their inspirations, good or bad.
- often get their facts slightly confused.
- dislike taking time for precision.

### Sensing Types—

- dislike new problems unless there are standard ways to solve them.
- like an established routine.
- enjoy using skills already learned more than learning new ones.
- work more steadily, with realistic ideas of how long it will take.
- must usually work all the way through to reach a conclusion.
- are impatient when situations get complicated.
- are patient with routine details.
- rarely trust inspirations and don't usually get inspired.
- seldom make errors of fact.
- tend to be good at precise work.

---

### Perceptive Types—

- tend to be good at adapting to changing situations.
- don't mind leaving things open for alterations.
- may have trouble making decisions.
- may start too many projects

### Judging Types—

- are at their best when they can plan their work and follow the plan.
- like to get things settled and cleanly finished.
- may decide things too quickly.

70

and have difficulty finishing them.
• may postpone unpleasant jobs.
• want to know all about a new job.
• tend to be curious and to welcome new light on a thing, situation, or person.

• may dislike interrupting the project they are on for a more urgent one.
• may not notice new things that need to be done.
• want only the essentials needed to do the work.
• tend to be satisfied once they reach a judgment on a thing, situation, or person.

---

You have found, I am sure, that the members of your family represent different combinations of preferences. This fact may be a clue to interpersonal relationships within the family. It can also help you solve problems and assist you and other family members in career searches.

In summary, a relationship exists between personality types and choices of career options—one that can provide success and satisfaction as opposed to failure and frustration. Use this knowledge as another tool to assist your children in their search for career options that will give them the life-style they want for themselves.

# 4

CIRCUMSTANCES
AND
YOUR PLANS

We all know people who have had to modify their plans as a result of circumstances that affected them. The economic depression during the 1930s ruined many people's plans; it also made some people millionaires. Circumstances can open up exciting new opportunities or they can devastate a life, depending on how they are approached. How one deals with circumstances depends on personal flexibility and powers of decision making.

Young people, having limited experience in dealing with circumstances, need assistance to become better able to cope with change. One way of helping them is to have them pretend to simulate the experience and thus plan how to deal with it. This allows them to think creatively of options available to them within the framework of the problem. The circumstances your children cope with in a role-playing situation are not likely to occur; however, the experience develops their ability to think more freely about other situations when they are faced with them. This activity continues the theme already suggested in this book: know who you are, know what is available, and then choose several options for yourself. Let us examine some methods of sharpening your children's skills at thinking of new options when circumstances must be dealt with.

To begin with, young people generally have optimistic plans for themselves. This is good, but changing circumstances can spoil those plans unless the young person has a chance to consider options, make a good choice, and then go on.

Many girls are suffering under the Cinderella myth—that is, though they say they want a career, they believe deep in their heart that a handsome, dashing young prince will carry them away from it all and that they will live happily ever after. As a result, sometimes their career plans fall by the wayside and they do not pursue the acquisition of employable skills. This is becoming less generally prevalent but unfortunately is still very evident in certain populations.

Many little girls, when asked what they want to do when they grow up, say, "Get married"—period. Yet data of the U.S. Department of Labor points out these interesting facts: The average life expectancy of women today is 75 years and, since childbearing patterns have changed, the average mother of today has forty years of life ahead of her after her youngest child has entered school. Nine out of ten girls will marry; eight out of ten will have children; one out of ten will be employed outside the home for some period of their lives; at least six out of ten will work full-time outside the home for up to thirty years; greater than one in ten will be widowed before age fifty; greater than one in ten will be heads of families; and probably three in ten will be divorced. Yet, according to a recent study only one in three girls plans to get some career training. Most girls do not see themselves as problem solvers or achievers, and many girls have not been trained to deal with the realities they will need to face in their lives. Society will continue to experience the loss of the talents of many bright women because they are not given early encouragement or are led to believe that they must choose between a family and a career. Do your daughters realize this?

Boys, on the other hand, often suffer under the myth that they will be rich and successful in a single career. But are they prepared to cope with some of the circumstances that affect men's lives? Not really.

Following are profiles of some real-life men and women, with some chance factors listed at the end of the segment. Before reading the chance factors, have your children read only the profile sections, choose one arbitrarily, work out their own life plan based on this information and their interests, aptitudes, and values as identified in earlier chapters of this book. You parents should choose one profile also; but in outlining your plan, take yourself back to the time when you were sixteen and try to remember what your plans were at that time.

74

This is an appropriate exercise for young people of fifteen years of age and older. Remember not to read the chance factors at the end of the profile section until after each of you has formulated a plan and shared it with the others. After you have done this, go back and read aloud the chance factors for each of the selected profiles in turn. After each reading, all family members should help the one who chose that profile think of new options to fit the circumstances, and at the same time, help modify or attempt to reach the original goal. After several options are presented, ask the person, "What would you probably do, based on your values, interests, skills, and personality?" Help her or him decide, going through the decision-making process as outlined below. It is also interesting to try this exercise with some of your children's friends.

Here is a model for decision making that can be used for any decision. In this particular activity the first step, identification of the problem, is already more or less completed for you.

## A Model for Decision Making

### Step One—The Problem

In this exercise the problem is: What shall I do with the rest of my life? The problem for another situation could be: Should I go to school or go to work? Shall I get married? Shall I order filet of fish or steak? But in any decision you must always first identify the problem.

### Step Two—Options

Once you have sized up a situation and feel the need to consider a change, the next step is to think of options. In this activity all of you will help each other think of options. Other people can help you in this step also; you may find that they can suggest options, you had not considered. Write these options down.

### Step Three—Probable Outcomes

You cannot know exactly what to expect from each option, but you can make an educated guess as to its outcome. The whole family can help in this step. Because of your varying experiences, not only can parents help children but children can help parents. You might find this to be so helpful that you will want to use the process for other decisions.

### Step Four—Values

In the final analysis, a person makes the choice he does because he values one thing more than another. You all identified some of your values in exercises in chapter two; go back to them now and refresh your memory. Your values involve how you feel about yourself; how you feel about others; your moral, ethnic, and religious beliefs; your emotional needs; and your motivations. You must weigh these values in making a decision. Although family members can point out any conflicts or discrepancies, each person must make his or her own decision. Others can provide perceptions and feelings, but the decision is the individual's. You as parents can say that you are disappointed with your child's decision, but you cannot force a decision based on your values.

### Step Five—Priorities

Now that you have each looked at your values and know what difference they will make in your final decision, go back and look at your options. Working individually, put them in order in terms of your values, looking also at the outcomes in light of your values.

### Step Six—Making a Decision

This step is obvious: make a decision and be sure you know exactly what it is.

### Step Seven—Action

A decision is not a decision until an action is taken. For this activity no action is required because it is a hypothetical decision; but in a real decision, action *must* be taken. The family should support each member in her or his decision and assist in the action if needed.

The following set of profiles and chance factors is for only the girls in your family to choose from, although the boys may offer counsel to them at the appropriate time. The profiles and chance factors for the boys follow those for the girls.

## When I Grow Up I'm Going To Be Married
## (For Girls)

### Profile No. 1

You will live to be seventy-five years old. You will marry and have children. You will work outside the home for some period during your life. You will not go to college before your marriage.

76

### Profile No. 2

You will live to be seventy-five years old. You will marry and have children. You will work outside the home for some period during your life. You will complete your college education before marriage.

### Profile No. 3

You will live to be seventy-five years old. You will marry and have children. You will work outside the home for some period during your life. You will not go to college before your marriage.

### Profile No. 4

You will live to be seventy-five years old. You will marry and have children. You will work outside the home for some period during your life. You will not go to college before your marriage.

### Profile No. 5

You will live to be seventy-five years old. You will marry and have children. You will work outside the home for some period in your life. You will complete two years of college before your marriage.

### Profile No. 6

You will live to be seventy-five years old. You will marry. You will work outside the home for some period during your life. You will not go to college before your marriage.

### Profile No. 7

You will live to be seventy-five years old. You will marry and have children. You will work outside the home for some period during your life. You will not go to college before your marriage.

### Profile No. 8

You will live to be seventy-five years old. You will marry and have children. You will not go to college before your marriage.

### Profile No. 9

You will live to be seventy-five years old. You will not go to college before taking your first job.

### Profile No. 10

You will live to be seventy-five years old. You will marry and have children. You will work outside the home for some period in your life. You will complete three years of college before your marriage.

When each of you has worked out a life plan based on one of the profiles above, turn to the chance factors for each profile and find out what the circumstances are in your simulated life. Each member of the family in turn should counsel the person whose "life" is affected as to how to resolve the conflicts presented.

### Chance Factors for Profile No. 1

You work as a secretary for two years before your marriage. You have two children. Your husband's job seems promising, but he does not advance as quickly as he hoped; and when the children are seven and nine you and he realize that, with the high cost of medical and dental care, taxes, college funds for the children, and the cost of a new home, one salary just will not do it.

What do you do?

### Chance Factors for Profile No. 2

You "fall into" the perfect job soon after graduation from college, and two years later meet and marry a young man with a promising future in a field other than yours. You keep on working after your two children are born because you love your work and are rising fast in your company. Ten years later, when you are near the top, your company is bought outright by a large conglomerate that plans to move the whole firm to New York. You are offered the directorship. There are no opportunities for you at your level if you switch to another company in your field in the town where you live. Opportunities for your husband in New York are unknown.

How do you approach this situation?

### Chance Factors for Profile No. 3

You work a year and are married at nineteen. You enjoy your twenty years of homemaking, but when you are forty your children are all grown. You do not want to sit at home for another thirty-five years.

What can you do?

### Chance Factors for Profile No. 4

You go to work for the telephone company when you are

eighteen. Two years later you marry a handsome, dashing line repairman, and by the time you are twenty-six you have three children. Your husband is assigned to emergency repair work in remote places, is home less and less, starts playing around with other women, and does not send money home regularly for you and the family. You try for three years to straighten things out; but by the time you reach thirty things are worse rather than better, and you get a divorce. The court awards you some spousal support alimony and child support, but it is not enough to live on, and there is very little community property—mostly just clothing and furniture.

How can you cope?

### Chance Factors for Profile No. 5

You have three children. Your husband has a good job and things are going well for the family until you are thirty-four, when your husband is tragically killed in an automobile accident. The children are then four, eight, and ten. There is some life insurance, but not enough to last very long.

How will you cope?

### Chance Factors for Profile No. 6

You marry your high school "steady" right after you graduate from high school. He has completed two years of college at that point, and you go to work as a clerk-typist in a law firm to help put him through school. He graduates and gets a good job. After five years in the law firm you are promoted to head secretary. It is fascinating work; and, while you and your husband are disappointed that no children have come along, you decide that since you both enjoy the challenges and freedom of your life you will not adopt children. You are very interested in the cases being handled by the firm, but over the next fifteen years you find that your secretarial role is less and less challenging. You are thirty-eight.

What will you do with the rest of your life?

### Chance Factors for Profile No. 7

It becomes apparent within two years that your marriage was a mistake and you are divorced. You remarry when you are twenty-four and have two children. When you are thirty-five and the children are seven and nine, your husband's job and whole field of work are wiped out by automation.

How can the family cope?

## Chance Factors for Profile No. 8

In your senior year in high school you fall madly in love with an exciting "older man," aged twenty-nine, who is already successful in business. He is of the firm opinion that woman's place is in the home and states often that no wife of his will ever work. The two of you continue to be generally compatible and remain married all your lives, but over the years his business affairs take up more and more of his time, and he prefers spending his leisure time hunting and fishing "with the boys." Your children are all off on their own by the time you are forty-three years old.

What do you do with the rest of your life?

## Chance Factors for Profile No. 9

Your father dies unexpectedly when you are seventeen and your mother is in poor health. You have four younger brothers and sisters, the youngest two years old, and supporting the family is up to you. You have no practical skills and jobs are scarce, but you get work in a cleaning plant. The pay is not bad, but you are tired by nighttime, especially after taking care of things at home. You have boyfriends, but the ones you really like have their own problems and do not want to take over support of your family. By the time the other children can help out enough so that most of your earnings are not needed for the family, you are thirty-five years old. You find that at that age there are very few eligible men around. You never do find one.

What will you do with the rest of your life?

## Chance Factors for Profile No. 10

Your fiance graduates from college as you finish your junior year and is offered a good job in a town that has no four-year college. You marry and go with him. When you are forty-two, and your children are fifteen and seventeen, your husband says he wants a divorce to marry a younger woman. Under California's new divorce law (effective in 1970) he can do this and there is nothing you can do about it. The new law also says you cannot get spousal support merely because you are a woman; but since you have been married for such a long time the court awards you a small amount of spousal support for three years and child care support until the children reach age twenty-one. You also get one of the cars and the furniture, all paid, and the house, only two-thirds paid. Even with the support money there is not going to be enough to make ends meet.

How will you cope?

Following are the profiles and the chance factors for seventeen other simulated life situations. These are intended for use by the male members of your family. As before, read only the profiles for the first part of the exercise. After each person has finished detailing a life plan based on the profile he is using, turn to the chance factors for that profile.

## When I Grow Up I'm Going To Be Rich
## (For Boys)

### Profile No. 1

You will live to seventy-one years old. You will marry and have children. You will go to college before your marriage. You will work most of your life.

### Profile No. 2

You will live to be seventy-one years old. You will marry and have children. You will complete college and medical school after your marriage.

### Profile No. 3

You will live to be seventy-one years old. You will marry and have no children. You will go into military service directly after high school. You will complete two years of college before your marriage.

### Profile No. 4

You will live to be seventy-one years old. You will marry and have children. You will start working directly after high school. You will not go to college before your marriage.

### Profile No. 5

You will live to be seventy-one years old. You will marry and have children. You will start working directly after high school. You will marry soon after high school graduation.

81

### Profile No. 6

You will live to be seventy-one years old. You will marry and have children. You will go to college before your marriage.

### Profile No. 7

You will live to be seventy-one years old. You will marry and have children. You will go to college directly after high school.

### Profile No. 8

You will live to be seventy-one years old. You will marry and have children. You will start working directly after high school. You will not go to college before your marriage.

### Profile No. 9

You will live to be seventy-one years old. You will marry and have children. You will start working directly after high school. You will not go to college before your marriage.

### Profile No. 10

You will live to be seventy-one years old. You will marry after you start college. You will start work directly after high school.

### Profile No. 11

You will live to be seventy-one years old. You will marry and have children. You will start working directly after high school.

### Profile No. 12

You will live to be seventy-one years old. You will marry and have children. You will go to college directly after high school. You will go to college before your marriage.

### Profile No. 13

You will live to be seventy-one years old. You will not marry. You will go to work directly after high school.

### Profile No. 14

You will live to be seventy-one years old. You will marry and have children. You will go to college directly after high school. You will complete college.

### Profile No. 15

You will live to be seventy-one years old. You will marry while in college and have children. You will work for a year after high school to save money and then go on to college.

### Profile No. 16

You will live to be seventy-one years old. You will marry and have no children. You will go to college directly after high school.

### Profile No. 17

You will live to be seventy-one years old. You will marry after college graduation. You will go to college directly after high school. You will complete college.

Now, as before, turn to the chance factors in these simulated lives to find out what situations each of you will have to deal with in your discussions.

### Chance Factors for Profile No. 1

You get married during college. You have three children and live a comfortable life, attending night school, and eventually finding work as a treasurer for a jewelry firm. An exciting job is offered to you: treasurer of a travel firm. You accept it because of the free travel benefits. Now two of your three children are in college, and the youngest will start next year. Economic conditions change; people are not traveling anymore. Your business, which caters to low-cost travel, has to lay you off due to a lack of business. You are left with mortage payments, your children's education, and a damaged self-concept.

What do you do?

### Chance Factors for Profile No. 2

You are a straight-A student and go to the medical school of your choice. As a junior you meet and marry an occupational therapist, and she works while you attend medical school. You have two children and spend six months in the Coast Guard, but leave because you do not like the restrictions. You go into private practice and buy an expensive home. At the age of forty-five, you have a complete mental breakdown from exhaustion and realize that you do not like being a doctor. You have always secretly wanted to be a stockbroker.

What will you do?

## Chance Factors for Profile No. 3

You complete two years of military service, then go to college on the G.I. bill. After two years you get married to an older woman who is in the residency stage of her medical career. You are in a four-year computer science program. You both complete your education and in five more years you share your ideal lifestyle. You have an expensively furnished home and own two sports cars, and you travel and entertain in accordance with your positions. You realize that you have large debts but count on your combined incomes (yours is $29,000, hers $38,000) to see you through. Then your wife has a disastrous car accident, can no longer work, and needs full-time home nursing care.

How will you cope?

## Chance Factors for Profile No. 4

You get a job immediately after high school. You marry and have two children. You lose two jobs due to lack of skills and job phase-out. You go to a night technical school but due to the employment situation cannot find employment in your new field.

What do you do?

## Chance Factors for Profile No. 5

You get a job in a mill right after high school and marry your high school sweetheart. A year later you have one child. After working three years you find that you are very dissatisfied with your job and feel that there is no more room for advancement, so you quit and begin looking for another. You feel lucky to be hired as an apprentice dye maker, and at the same time you go to school to become a design engineer. You get a good job as a draftsman and work your way up in the business as a design engineer. You work for twenty years; then the owners decide to move the business to a new city. You are not ready to retire, but are not really anxious to move.

How do you approach the situation?

## Chance Factors for Profile No. 6

In college you meet and marry a girl who is studying to be a nurse. You get a degree in education and get a job teaching elementary school; your wife quits school and you have three children. You work as a teacher for ten years and get a master's degree in education administration by going to night school. You become principal of a small elementary school, but your philosophy is very different from that of your superintendent and you have many conflicts. Eventually you are placed back in the classroom. You are discouraged and so your teaching suffers. A child of one of the board members is in your class and complains a great deal about how you teach. This board member convinces the other board members that you are incompetent and you are fired even though you have tenure. You appeal the case through the State Teachers' Association but lose. Your children are aged eight, fifteen, and seventeen, and you are paying on a house. You are forty-six years old. You cannot get another teaching job because of your work history and the overcrowded labor market.

What do you do?

### Chance Factors for Profile No. 7

You go to college and then to graduate school; while in graduate school you marry. Both you and your wife are graduate students and you support yourselves with part-time jobs and fellowships. After you get your graduate degrees you each get a job in your respective fields. You have two children. Your wife continues working and becomes an increasingly effective member of a research team with growing responsibilities and satisfaction. You live in a lovely house overlooking the ocean and your children are well settled and thriving in their school. Then your firm offers you a challenging and exciting job heading a new project at the opposite side of the country. You would love the chance to supervise the development of a new idea.

How do you handle this?

### Chance Factors for Profile No. 8

You apprentice yourself to a skilled craftsman. His business expands and your job with it, and you make a very good living. You become the owner's partner; when he dies, you become sole owner. You live in a large house, your children are in private schools, and you have a very high standard of living but no savings. A depression hits and your business plummets.

What do you do?

### Chance Factors for Profile No. 9

You join the army directly after high school, find the life satisfying, and decide to make it your career. Through the training and educational opportunities you earn ninety college credits. You marry and have two children. Your assignments take you all over the world and you and your family move on the average of every two years. After twenty years, when you are thirty-nine, you are eligible for retirement at two-thirds pay with continued medical benefits and commissary rights.

What do you do?

## Chance Factors for Profile No. 10

You do not know what you want to do or where you want to live. You spend two years working at odd jobs at various places around the country. You like where you are after two years—you like the people and the way of life. There is a good community college and you begin taking courses. It takes some time, as you are working full-time, but you eventually complete a program preparing you for a field that interests you and receive an associate degree. You are hired by a local firm and do well. You marry a local girl and settle into the community. The president of your company then decides to open a new division in a different section of the United States and wants to send you there. You would enjoy the challenge, but your wife has always lived in the area where you are now and does not want to leave her family and friends.

How do you handle this?

## Chance Factors for Profile No. 11

You find employment with the county government. The pay seems good and you marry the girl you were dating in your last couple of years of high school. Small annual salary increases help to meet the rising expenses as two children arrive. After six years, you are twenty-four years old and are supporting a wife and two children aged three and four. Your job is quite routine and with no further education there is little chance for advancement. You are becoming increasingly bored and frustrated. Both you and your wife worry over the difficulty of affording necessities and desire to have the financial freedom that would allow for a few extras.

What kind of solution do you find?

## Chance Factors for Profile No. 12

You go to college, but after a year and a half you drop out and go to work. In order to supplement your income you join the

86

Naval Reserve. You marry and have one child. Through on-the-job training and trade school courses, you become a highly skilled and well-paid craftsman in a trade requiring a great deal of physical coordination and the use of your hands. Then a world crisis results in your Naval Reserve unit being called into active duty. You are wounded, retired on fifty percent disability, and must find some other kind of work. Your wife is a high school graduate and has never worked. Your child is five years old.

### Chance Factors for Profile No. 13

Your father has a successful business and persuades you to work for him directly after high school. He anticipates that you will eventually take over the business; and as he developed the business without a college education, he does not think you need one. There are other things you would rather do and you would like to go on to college, but he is very insistent and offers you a good salary, so you agree. You become interested in learning the business and fifteen years go by. You enjoy your way of life and have many outside interests. However, you become increasingly restless as your father keeps a tight rein on the business.

What do you do?

### Chance Factors for Profile No. 14

You complete college and work in a job you enjoy—however it does not pay very well. You marry and have two children. Your wife does not work, but through careful handling of your money you manage to live comfortably. Your marriage is not a happy one—there is increasing dissension and misery. Finally you agree to divorce. You live in a state where you must pay spousal support and child care support, and you find yourself financing two households. You manage to scrape by for a while, but after a few years you want to marry again.

How do you handle this?

### Chance Factors for Profile No. 15

Your wife works to support you while you finish college. After graduation you get a job in the field you have chosen and your wife continues working while you save to buy a house. When she becomes pregnant, she stops working and changes her role to that of homemaker and mother. You work in your field for twenty years and do well. Much of your work you enjoy; however, it is very competitive and there is constant pressure and stress from constantly trying to gain over the competition. In your forties, you gradually become very tired of the pressure and find that those aspects you had enjoyed have become stale and repetitive. You would like to do something else. However, you are supporting a high standard of living which you, your wife, and your children are all accustomed to enjoying.

What can you do?

### Chance Factors for Profile No. 16

You go to college directly after high school. Unfortunately, you become overly involved in social and extracurricular activities and flunk out. You work for a couple of years but find your job routine and unsatisfying and wish to return to college. Your family feels that you are now financially on your own, so you attend a local community college part-time while working and do well. You enter a field you enjoy, but it involves long and irregular hours. You marry and, though your wife would like children, you do not have any. She is quite dependent and enjoys the role of wife and homemaker, but she becomes increasingly unhappy and depressed at being alone so much.

How do you handle this?

### Chance Factors for Profile No. 17

After college you attend graduate school and obtain a master's degree in your field. You get a good job with a company and progress well. You marry and have three children. Your wife does not work. Suddenly the product your company makes becomes obsolete and the company goes into bankruptcy. You are without a job and there is no demand for your specialized training.

What do you do?

Do these lives sound depressing? Such things do happen, however, and the state of mind with which you deal with these problems will affect your life satisfaction. Here are some examples of how other people are coping with circumstances.

Ben Fields, 24, is a Phi Beta Kappa graduate with a degree in psychology from a well-known eastern university. He subsists on food stamps and unemployment compensation. He has had one response to the fifty resumes he sent out, but he did not get the job.

Joe Alvin, 30, has a job as an office boy for a real estate firm. He has also been a cab driver and has worked in a service station. He has a Ph.D. in philosophy from one of the "big ten" schools.

Young people with degrees in foreign languages, English, and psychology as well as those with advanced degrees are working as liquor clerks, bank tellers, filing clerks, cab drivers, and farm hands. Have they made the right decisions? Who knows? But, whether appropriately or inappropriately, they have had to cope with circumstances they did not anticipate.

One problem young people will have to face is the compatibility of a career and a family. Although working couples have always faced this decision, opening options for women may engender even greater strains on families. It is a good idea to discuss this question with your teenagers or older children. Ask the following questions and discuss them as a family.

1. Do you plan to marry? Why?
2. At what age do you plan to marry? Why?
3. Do you want children? Why? How Many?
4. If a boy, do you want your wife to work? Why? What if she makes more money than you?
5. If a girl, do you want your husband to make more or less money than you, or does it matter?
6. Whose career will be primary? That is, if one person is transferred, whose career takes precedence?
7. Do you think these questions sould be discussed before marriage?
8. Are there some career combinations that would be incompatible to the best interests of the children?

A young couple I know have had to make a decision involving many of these questions. She is a researcher working in New York City and has an apartment in Manhattan. He is a professor at the University of Ohio, and they have a home in Columbus, Ohio. He cannot find a comparable job in New York; she cannot find one in Columbus. They have decided that they should not have children, though originally they had wanted two, because they feel that their way of life would not be suitable to a family. Many other couples are facing the same problem. They must make decisions, but first must have clearly in mind their values and the kind of life-style they want as well as what career options

89

to choose. What do you and your children think of the situation? How will your children cope? Talk about it.

To make sure you understand the decision-making process, each of you could write down some decision that you have to make soon, go through the process as a family with each one, and help each other arrive at a decision.

### Culminating Activity

To emphasize the fact that decisions you make affect many parts of your life, think of a major decision you have made in your life and write it down.

Now imagine what your life would be like if you had chosen one of the other options:

How would your day be different?

How would the way you spend your leisure time be different?

How would your family be different?

How would your life-style be different?

Would your career be different?

What decisions would you probably have to be making right now?

What decisions are you now making that you would not have to make?

Discuss your responses. Do you find that your life-style might be considerably different than it is? This is probably more true for adults than for children. This activity is just one more indication that knowing how to make decisions is important. It is a process you will be using for the rest of your life.

*Outline of Resume*

NAME
ADDRESS
TELEPHONE

JOB OBJECTIVE:

State type of job sought with the company, For example: A beginning job in _____, leading to a position in _____.

EDUCATION:

Names of schools and years attended, degrees held, major

subject field, special courses, awards and citations. (If there is space, list of courses related to the job sought.)

## EXTRACURRICULAR ACTIVITIES OR OUTSIDE INTERESTS:
School and club activities, hobbies, or other outside interests with direct or tangential bearing on job objective.

## EXPERIENCE:
All full-time, part-time, summer, or volunteer jobs held, and explanation of how this work experience (limited though it may be) has valuable application to present job objective and future vocational goal.

Usable work skills acquired both in and out of school: typing, operating business machines, fluency in foreign languages, etc.

## PERSONAL DATA:
Date of birth _____     Health _____
Height _____     Marital Status _____
Weight _____

REFERENCES: List of three, or the statement, "Available upon Request."

*Sample Resume*

### NAME
### ADDRESS
### TELEPHONE

OBJECTIVE:     Part-time work (after school hours and/or weekends) as copy person or in similar capacity in newspaper office, hoping eventually to enter professional field in reporting.

EDUCATION:     Presently in sophomore year at New York University. Major in journalism, minor in music. Secretary of Student Council; member of Publications Committee and Student Music Staff.

Graduated Blair High School, Brooklyn, N.Y.,

June 1967. Seventh in class of 360; winner of creative writing medal.

Extracurricular activities included active membership in Journalism Club, Photography Workshop, Spanish Club. Library aide for three years.

WORK SKILLS: Typing: 60 w.p.m.
Office machine operation: mimeograph, rexograph, ditto.
Production: page layout, mechanicals, paste-up, scaling and retouching of photographs.

EMPLOYMENT: Summers, 1965, 1966: Newspaper route on commission basis.
Summers, 1967, 1968: Caddy, Lido Golf Club, Westchester.

PERSONAL: Born: August 16, 1950.
Height: 5' 11"; Weight: 167 lbs.; Health: Excellent.
Hobbies: Photo buff; do own developing and printing. Write short stories (unpublished).

Mother is author of series of children's books.
Father, now deceased, was well-known sports photographer.

REMARKS: Salary secondary in importance to opportunity to be and work in atmosphere of editorial department of large city newspaper.

REFERENCES: School and personal references when required.

# 5

## THE
## VALUE
## OF WORK

Many parents protect their children from the work environment for as long as possible, believing that they are helping them by allowing them to enjoy their childhood without the responsibility of work. Actually, children are done a disservice by not being allowed early experience with the work world.

How can parents motivate young people to work? Not providing unlimited spending money will provide motivation for some. Occasionally parents misinterpret certain behaviors and conclude that their children are lazy when actually they are only fearful of the thought of looking for and holding a job. Having chores to do at home is an excellent introduction to work.

Some chores should be done without pay. "We all have to do some things to keep the household going" is a good rationale for this. Chores should begin at very young ages. To avoid hostilities, these jobs can be rotated and sex-stereotyping avoided. No jobs should be considered "boy's work" or "girl's work"; all children should learn life-coping skills such as cooking, cleaning, planning menus, raking leaves, mowing grass and so on. In addition to providing a healthy attitude toward work, these skills can be used later in volunteer and paying jobs, which can in turn be listed in a resume.

By the time children are twelve, they should at least have been encouraged to think about working. Children of junior high school age are too young to hold regular paying jobs in a business or industry, but they can do volunteer work or find work around the neighborhood. This is also an excellent introduction to work. Volunteer service can include assisting in a Sunday school class, Cub Scouts, Girl Scouts, Blue Birds, 4H, or other organizations, and can be used as work experience when applying for a paying job. From it, young people learn good work attitudes and a sense of responsibility. They should definitely get a letter of recommendation from their supervisor (Girl Scout leader, Sunday school teacher, etc.) while still working in the job. Sometimes, such people have not been asked to give recommendations in the past and may need help. You could give them a form to fill out if you wish. Here is an example:

Name
Work attitudes (punctuality, etc.)
Acceptance of responsibilities
Relationship with other workers and people served
Skills utilized on the job
Comments

If young people know before starting work that the adult in charge will be asked to give an evaluation and if they know what areas will be evaluated, they will be more careful workers. Discuss this with them before they begin their volunteer or paid work.

Enterprising children between the ages of ten and fourteen can usually find work around the neighborhood or apartment building doing ironing, cleaning, dog washing and walking, yard work, child care, animal care, hauling trash, shoveling snow, and so forth. They could print several three-by-five cards with name, phone number, and a list of jobs they can do and give them to neighbors. This is a good beginning to learning job-seeking skills.

One ten-year old girl asked her parents if she could have a gymnastic mat. Her parents asked her how much money she had; five dollars, she answered. Her parents then asked how much a mat cost. The girl had to call several stores and do some comparative shopping to answer. The mat she wanted cost forty-five dollars. Her mother said, "I guess you will have to get a job." The girl's enthusiasm waned, but with the encouragement of her parents, she decided to run a "mother's-helper children's group" for three- to six-year-olds on summer mornings from nine to twelve in partnership with another girl her age. They gave out cards to all the neighbors with young children, and their business began to thrive. In three weeks they had enough money to buy the mat. The girls then discontinued their service, but they had learned a great deal from the experience and probably appreciated their money more than they would have had it been given to them.

Developing hobbies is important for children also. Hobbies sometimes work into paying jobs or provide satisfactions that jobs do not.

Usually at about age fourteen or fifteen children are ready to branch out from neighborhood jobs. Some service stations, fast-food establishments, and day-care centers will hire young people under sixteen years old. The young people then need a work permit, obtainable from the junior or senior high school counselor or administrator, and a social security number. The social security form can also be obtained from the school.

As parents, you will probably have to provide transportation during these first years, and there will be times when you will wonder whether or not it is worth it. It is. The experience is valuable, and it is your responsibility as a parent to encourage your children to work at this age. They should be charged a minimum amount for the transportation you supply; this is only realistic. If you decide it is not worth it, you can blame no one but yourself when your eighteen- or nineteen-year-old refuses to work. It is a big step from working for neighbors and nonpaying organizations to working for a business for money. Your children will need help to make this change. Their reluctance should not necessarily be interpreted as laziness; it could be fear. Give them the benefit of the doubt—try to remember how you felt.

It will help to discuss with them questions they might be asked. Of course, experience from volunteer jobs and neighborhood jobs and a letter of recommendation or two will also help. Some questions they might be asked are:

"Why do you want to work?"

Although "I need money" is a passable answer, this is better: "I want more work experience and I also find that I need more money." This expresses more willingness to learn.

"Why do you want to work for us?"

A good answer to this would be: "I've noticed what the workers here do and I believe that I would enjoy working for you."

"Why should we hire you?"

"I don't know" is not a good answer. The employer can probably get along very nicely without workers who do not know why they should be hired. A better response is: "Because I'm a good worker and I'm responsible. I think I could do a good job."

These are, of course, only samples. They should be expressed in the young person's own words to reflect the same general idea.

If the employer says, "We don't need anyone right now, but we'll call you if we do," the chances are that he or she will not.

An appropriate response is, "May I have your number to call you back in a week or so? There is often no one at home to answer the phone." Then you can call them back, several times if necessary.

To illustrate another creative response, here is a true story. A sixteen-year-old girl was applying for a job at a local fast-food chain. From ages ten to twelve, she had babysat for neighbors' children. At thirteen she had worked as a volunteer in a day-care center for the mentally retarded and had a letter of recommendation from a supervisor there. At fourteen she had worked for pay at a day-care center during the summer in addition to cleaning and ironing during the school year. She had a letter of recommendation from each place of employment.

At fifteen she worked in a family restaurant serving coffee and soft drinks. She was energetic and friendly in her work and got more tips than any other waitress. She had a letter of recommendation from there also. When the restaurant closed, she decided to apply at this fast-food spot close to home. The employer told her to fill out an application even though they did not need anyone right now, and she suggested, "Perhaps you would like to look at my letters of recommendation while I'm filling out the application."

The employer read the letters and exclaimed, "Say, you sound pretty good! Come back Wednesday and I'll give you a job." If she had left after he said he had no position, she might never have been hired. Places that have a large volume of applicants generally hire the first person that impresses them when they have an immediate job opening.

The above story illustrates several important job-seeking skills applicable not only to teenagers but to adults as well. One is to get a letter of recommendation while in good standing and from the most compatible supervisor. It is never safe to wait; the next supervisor may clash in personality and more readily give a bad recommendation. All one needs to say is, "I'm keeping my work experience file up to date." If desired the form recommended for volunteer work supervisors can be adapted for this purpose.

Although the previous pages were intended for those of junior and senior high school age, these same bits of advice can serve any adults lacking job-seeking skills. You parents can sharpen your job-seeking skills as well and assist your older children in their job search, or use them if, as a result of the value and interest activities in earlier chapters, you have decided that you want to change careers. You must first learn the rules of the job-getting game and then learn to break some of those rules.

## Letter of Application

The letter of application has several objectives to fulfill. First, it should interest the employer so that she or he will interview the applicant. Second, it should accompany either a resume or a completed application or both. Third, it should indicate some interest in the company. A carefully composed letter of application can make the difference between an employer passing the application on to the personnel office with a note saying, "This looks good," and his depositing it in the wastebasket. Here are some hints for writing one.

• Address the letter to the appropriate person in the firm, using his name.
• Use good quality 8½ x 11 white bond paper.
• Type the letter or have it typed.
• Be careful with spelling and punctuation.
• Be brief—make it no longer than one page.
• Focus on why you want to work for the firm and what contribution you can make.
• Refer to your resume but do not repeat it in full. Concentrate on parts of your resume that support the job for which you are applying.
• Suggest that you phone for an interview, then be sure to make the phone call within a week after mailing your letter.
• Keep a copy of all letters you send.

## The Application Blank

Filling out an application may seem quite elementary. Surprisingly enough, many adults who should know better make some disastrous mistakes when filling out an application. It is important to know how to fill out an application properly; in some cases it is the application that presents the employer with a first impression.

The primary function of the application form is to secure an interview; it should be filled out with this in mind. A good idea is to go over the completed form as if in the employer's place. Would he or she be interested as a result of this application? It is also a good idea to ask for two copies of the application in case anything needs to be changed.

Some employers will discard any applications that have unanswered questions. If any of the questions cannot be answered—for example, "maiden name" for a man—it is best to write "not applicable" or "NA" in that space.

Although certain questions are by regulation illegal, they still crop up in some application forms. Objecting to even an obviously sexist or discriminating question may perhaps win the point, but it will probably lose the job. It is a personal decision.

It should be obvious that the completed application ought to be neat and legible, but again it is amazing to see the condition of applications written by people who should know better.

Certain questions traditionally cause problems on applications. The important thing to keep in mind is, "I want the interview." On questions related to health, the answer should always be "excellent." One young man I know answered "fair" to this question. "I'm 40 pounds overweight and I'm taking medication for high blood pressure," he protested.

"How many days have you missed in the last two months?" I asked.

"None," he responded.

"Then you're healthier than I am. Put excellent or to be explained in interview instead."

The phrase "to be explained in interview" can be used for controlled diabetes or controlled epilepsy. Obviously, one should not lie on the application. On the other hand, there is no point in giving more information than is being demanded. The real question is, "Will this condition affect my performance on the job?" If it will not, the question should be answered accordingly.

The question, "Have you or any members of your family suffered from a mental disorder?" sometimes poses problems. If Grandmother suffered from a nervous breakdown in 1929, I personally believe that one can honestly answer no. "To be explained in interview" can also be used.

Can a person who was taking drugs in Viet Nam but has not had any for two years answer no to the question, "Have you or any members of your family received treatment for chemical dependency (alcohol or narcotics)?" Such a decision is an individual one, but the answer should never be simply yes.

Other problem questions may be "Do you use alcohol?" and "What is your father's vocation?" This latter is especially hard if he is in jail or is a racketeer. Employers have prejudices, and answers should be made accordingly. The individual must use common sense within her or his own value structure, remembering always that she or he wants an interview.

## The Resume

The object in writing a resume is to make the employer really want to see the applicant. It can be sent with the letter of application or application form. A resume takes a lot of thought and rewriting, but it is worth the trouble. By the time your children are about sixteen and have had two or three jobs, it is time to help them put their resumes together. Tell them also to keep them updated for the rest of their working life. Incidentally, do you have one?

A resume is a summary of one's background. A good one, however, is more than that: it is an advertisement of oneself. It should answer three questions employers want to know: What are the applicant's work skills? What are her work attitudes? What are his work habits? It should get the employer interested, at least to the extent of wanting an interview. The very act of writing a resume helps organize background and skills and gives one a better self-concept. It also assists in the interview. Skills such as those identified in the "excerpts from life" activity in chapter one can be used in the resume. You may have heard that "It's not what you know but who you know that's important in getting a job." To an extent this is true, but writing a good resume will assist in getting a job nonetheless. At first your children will have little experience. The examples of resumes given at the end of the chapter are for young people with little experience as well as those with more experience and education. They will want to change their resumes in content and emphasis as they gain experience.

Experts have differing opinions on what makes a good resume, but most agree on certain things: Employers want to make money or provide good service. They want things to run smoothly. A good resume makes use of this idea and stresses the applicant's interest in the employer. Unfavorable information should be omitted. This does not mean to lie, but it does mean not to make derogatory statements. If the applicant had difficulty getting along with a former supervisor, the resume does not need to mention it.

As with the application, a good question to ask oneself is: "If I were an employer, would I want to interview me on the basis of this resume?" If the answer is merely a shrug, the resume needs to be livened up and to have some negative things eliminated. Following is an outline of items to include:

Identification: Name, address, telephone number

Work wanted (Objective); Specific but without limiting chances to be considered for other openings (For instance, the applicant who can type, take shorthand, and complete receptionist duties should write, "secretarial or related position," not "office work." That would be too general.)

Education: Years attended, name and location of school, major course of study, and other courses related to the kind of work sought.

Work Experience: Employment dates (most recent employer first), types of work (Volunteer work is included here. Employers look for gaps in education and work, so the resume should be kept updated and should account for periods between education and work—travel, maternity leave, and so on. Military service is included in its proper sequence under "work experience." Each job should include a brief summary of the major tasks per formed.

## Making Contacts

The person who knows how to write a letter of application, fill out an application form, and update a resume is truly ready to look for work. But where? Sending hundreds of letters to prospective employers is a waste of time. However, want ads are a possibility. The yellow pages exercise in chapter two can provide a list of possible employers. Governmental agencies are another possibility.

It saves time and letters to call to determine if there are any openings at a business before sending a letter of application. When looking for a job, one should not be hesitant to use friends as sources of information and initial contacts, to let everybody

100

know about the job-hunt, and to follow up on all suggestions.

Anyone with a real desire to work with a certain agency or industry should not be afraid to follow up when told, "We're not hiring." Companies can usually find positions for people they really want. The key is to be assertive. Eating lunch in the company cafeteria so as to ask questions, study how the people dress, and listen to conversations is a good plan. One can also find out about departments that are particularly good to work for. In this preliminary contact it is not good to come on like a job hunter, but merely to show some interest in the company. Finding out who makes the decisions and learning something about this person will assist in the interview. It is also good to get as much information about the company and the people as possible so as to be able to respond confidently in the interview.

To find work in a particular geographic area where one knows nobody, it can be helpful to write to the chamber of commerce for a list of industries or to get a copy of the local paper and the yellow pages of the telephone directory to identify some possible prospects. Then, taking a two- or three-week vacation and making some contacts—not as a job hunter, but as someone who is interested in the community—you can obtain interviews with people unattainable to a job hunter. After an interview with someone such as the superintendent of schools in the district or the president of the local firm, it is good policy to send him or her a thank-you note within 24 hours; if you train your children to send thank-you notes, you have provided them with a good job-seeking skill.

An interview such as described above provides a contact in that area for future job-seeking. Many people who make these initial contacts as interested citizens rather than job hunters are then offered employment. If your children are seniors in high school or are in college, encourage them to develop these community contacts. It will pave the way for their job search later. However, if your children are ready for work now and cannot afford the luxury of this early contact exercise, they should then use all the resources listed previously to find possible openings: friends, relatives, trade magazines and journals, want ads, yellow pages, chambers of commerce, employment services, churches, and schools. Their former and present teachers or counselors are also a good resource. You and your children need to discover who in your town might know about job openings, and then follow up every possibility.

# The Interview

After having gone through the procedures on applications, resumes, and making contacts, your children are then ready to prepare for interviews. The interview is critical. Some things to remember and to prepare for are as follows:

The applicant must know what the company or agency does or produces. However one comes by this information, it is extremely important to have. It may make the difference.

How do the people who work there dress? It is a good idea to visit the company prior to the interview to observe how the people dress in order to dress accordingly for the interview. A woman applying for a job at Saks Fifth Avenue should look "Saks Fifth Avenue" rather than "Salvation Army store" when going for an interview. Makeup and jewelry are all part of the image. And as far as some companies are concerned it would be disastrous for a man to come to an interview dressed in a sports jacket, flowered shirt, and striped pants instead of a dark suit, white shirt, and plain tie. In an establishment where the workers wear uniforms, a simple, neat attire is advisable.

The applicant should know for what job he or she is applying and what that job involves and, if possible, something about the person or persons interviewing. If both employer and applicant are health-food enthusiasts, it would not hurt to subtly mention this interest in common. However, if the applicant thinks health-food enthusiasts are eccentric, mentioning it would not be tactful. One must use common sense, keeping in mind the question, "Would I hire me?"

When going into the interview, one should give a firm handshake and talk in a clear, strong voice, not being afraid to smile and maintaining good eye contact. Things to be sure to say and questions to ask can be jotted down on some three-by-five cards and held, not hidden, in the lap. They should not be read, but glanced at when needed to jolt the memory.

Parents, your children will need your help in preparing for the interview. Ask them questions and have them respond to you as they would to an employer. Then critique them on their responses: Are they positive? Are they clear? Are they too long? Are they concise? Are they on the subject? Do they leave the employer with a positive reaction? This is no time to be kind. Be frank and give your impressions, but in a constructive way—for example, "That response was a little long," not, "That was terrible! You should know better than that." Questions that may be asked follow:

"Where did you hear about the job?"

"I saw the ad in the newspaper and it immediately interested me" is a good response. An answer such as, "I saw your *little* ad in the newspaper" may seem like a put-down or a value judgement, and should be avoided.

"Tell me a little about yourself."

A brief educational and work history makes a good beginning; an outline of hobbies and interests could follow. These should give a positive impression of willingness to work and should not last longer than two minutes total.

"Why should I hire you?" or "How do you know you can do the job?"

The response to either of these questions should include one's skills, aptitudes, interests, and work values, not how desperately he or she needs a job. Vague statements of past successes are also out of place. Again, this response should be kept under two minutes, and preferably about one, in duration.

"How much money do you expect to make?"

If there is a quotation of the salary in the ad, it can be safely mentioned. It is best, under other circumstances, not to quote an exact figure either in the application or in the interview. "I'm sure the going rate for this position would be satisfactory; what is the salary for this position?" is a fine response—it neither prices one out of the position nor undersells one.

If the salary is not satisfactory, then salary negotiations may be in order. However, for an experienced worker a statement such as the following may be more appropriate than negotiation: "I was hoping for more. If I prove myself on the job, are there promotional opportunities?" This gives an impression of confidence that one's work will merit more.

A question often asked of young unmarried women is, "Are you planning to get married?"

A possible answer is, "It's none of your business." However, a response giving a more favorable impression is, "I don't have any plans for marriage at the present, but I am interested in a career; I'm sure I can combine marriage and a career if my plans change."

It is impossible to list all the problem questions that could be asked; the point to remember is to respond to them in a positive way. If, for instance, a young man had been under psychiatric care and put "to be explained in interview" on his application, he could make this positive statement during the interview when asked to explain: "I was under a great deal of pressure during my last year of training because my father had died. I felt I needed help, but now I'm on top of it and am ready to go to work."

If, during the interview, the interviewer opens the discussion to questions about the job, it is best to ask first those questions related to expected duties and responsibilities rather than those concerning coffee breaks, lunch hours, vacations, and retirement benefits. It is good to ask some questions, however; they may be written out if necessary. Since vacations and retirement are important, questions on the benefits provided by the company are appropriate, but they should wait until last. Other legitimate questions may concern hours, promotional opportunities, and specific duties to be performed.

One is seldom hired immediately after an interview. A more probable arrangement will be to "call you in a few days to let you know of our decision." A call-back technique is the best course; the job seeker who simply waits by the phone may never be called. At the close of the interview, one can say, "I have several other interviews and may be out much of the time; may I have your card and call you in three or four days?" Then one can call back and, if no decision has been made, call again—and again.

In some situations, the interview may be conducted by several people in a group. There is no reason to become flustered by this; the same rules apply for a panel interview as for a one-to-one interview. Remembering the people's names as they are introduced and referring to them by name when appropriate—not too many times, but at least once—can be impressive.

Now that we have examined some of the rules of job-seeking, let us discuss how to creatively break some of them. I have stated that learning about the company and impressing the interviewer are important. Any information one can find and use to enhance the chances of being hired is fair. Such creative assertiveness in the job search is illustrated in the following story.

A young man desperate for a job read one day about interviews to be given at a local industry for a job he was qualified to perform. He checked the company out and went there to see how the employees dressed. On the day of the interview he arrived one-half hour early—to be sure to be on time, only to find twenty-five others in line ahead of him. Disappointed, he wondered what to do to stand out in that crowd. Finally, he wrote a note to the interviewer and took it to the receptionist, telling her it was urgent that she give the note to the interviewer. When the interviewing was over, he was hired for the job. The note had said, "My name is Bob Smith. I'm twenty-sixth in the line outside. Don't hire anyone until you've interviewed me."

The job-seeking rules say to fill out an application, file it with the personnel office, and wait—and wait—and wait, making no other contact with the company. But a person looking for a job in, say, accounting who can get an interview with the director of that department of an establishment should do it. The chances of getting a job are much better with an interview at this level. It is all right for friends and relatives to intercede—almost anything is fair in love and job hunting. Once hired, of course, a person must earn the right to keep the job, justifying the confidence of those who helped find it by doing the best work possible.

The following story illustrates this point. A woman trained as a nurse was working as an instructional aide in a large school system. She heard of a position that she wanted and felt qualified for, and she, along with thirty-nine others, applied for the one position through the personnel office and waited to be called. She received a form letter saying that she had been screened out ("paper screened," in the terminology of personnel offices) from the interviews. She was angry and, calling the principal of the school where the open position was, she said, "I'm not being allowed to interview for this job even though I feel I'm extremely qualified. I have ideas of how I could improve the services [she had done some research] and how the system can run more smoothly. I'd like at least to have an interview." She got not only the interview but the job as well.

The point made here is to think creatively of ways to work within the system and not to allow it to maintain control of your children's lives. As a family you can brainstorm ways in which your children can increase their chances of getting jobs. And after your children have a little experience, it may be appropriate for them to modify the job search even further. They have made contacts; they have identified further what job they want in what company to provide them with the life-style they want. Why should they deal through the personnel office at all? It may be better to figure out who the decision maker is, figure out what problems the company has (several days of eating lunch in the company cafeteria and listening and talking to employees will help here, even to finding out what golf course the boss frequents), marshal the skills necessary to solve them, and then make a contact. A knowledge, through research, of the company's problems and ideas on how to solve them can help one to know exactly what to say at a "chance" meeting at the golf course. The boss may not hire on the spot, but chances are that he or she will remember when the time comes for sorting applications, interviewing, and hiring.

Not everyone can effect a contact so boldly. Each person has to behave in a way consistent with his or her personality. Your children will need to modify these suggestions to fit their individual values, but in talking about them as a family you can probably think of some creative and common-sense ways to help each other along.

# 6

## THE PROBLEM WITH SCHOOLS

Schools were designed to help prepare children to live a life. Unfortunately, somewhere along the line this objective seems to have become unclear. Many young people are questioning the purpose of school, or at least the purpose of some of the courses they are required to take and the relevance they have to life—and in particular to the portion of their life that will be devoted to work. Some teachers have attempted to relate their subjects to life-styles, but in the event that your children have not had this advantage, it is for you to help them see the relationship between school and living.

The self-concept your children develop will affect their success in school and work. Many parents are unaware of how much the very early years at home and at school affect this self-concept. Many parents are also unaware of the role they have in determining the education their children receive.

One of the most damaging effects on the self-concept is failure. Among the places where many children first encounter failure are kindergarten and first grade. This does not mean failure to pass to the next grade, but rather the development of the distinct idea that they are not quite on the level of the rest of the students or are having more difficulty than others. If a child is not ready for school he or she will undoubtedly experience these feelings of failure, and many bright children are not ready for school. Placing them in school before they are ready affects their self-concept which, in turn, affects future school and work success.

107

As a parent, you have the right to keep your child out of school until he or she is ready. Such a decision could affect the child's future life. Your child may not be ready for school if he or she

• seems immature in comparison to other children of the same age.
• prefers to play with younger children.
• does not want to go to school (children often feel intuitively that they are unready).
• "is very bright," according to nursery school teachers, but seems a little immature.
• was born between June and December 1. December 1 is the cut-off date for school entrance in many states.

If you are uncertain about sending your child to school, read the book, *Is Your Child in the Wrong Grade?* for further information.[8]

Keeping your child out of school for a year could have a positive effect on his or her entire life. Parents often are discouraged by teachers and principals from keeping their children out of school, but if you feel strongly that they are unready, stand firm.

If your child is already in school and is at the bottom of the class even though she or he seems to be at least average in intelligence, try having her or him kept back—not failed, but kept back. This can be done in a positive way; perhaps you, the teacher, and the administrator could work out a plan whereby your child could be selected as a teacher's helper in the grade she or he has just finished. This can work wonders for the self-concept of the child. If you are reluctant to ask for this, or if the school is cool to the suggestion, remind yourself, "Schools were designed for children. I'm a taxpayer, and this decision could affect my child's entire life."

Other courses parents, children, and schools (remember that this is a team decision, at least on the part of children and parents) have chosen are for the child

• to stay an extra year in elementary school as a sixth-grade helper or library or office aide.
• to stay an extra year in junior high, taking other electives and working in the office or library.
• to work a year after senior high before going on to some post-high school training or education.

If parents and teachers work together and approach the child in a positive way this can be accomplished with success.

Some children manage to struggle through until the fourth grade and then seem to flounder. This is the time, then, to give the child an extra year of development. If your child becomes disinterested in school in the junior or senior high years and grades drop—a fairly typical occurrence—that is the time to initiate or reinitiate the activities given earlier in this book. The point is for children to realize how their behavior can affect the rest of their life. If children see no relationship between some of the courses they are taking and what they are going to do, grades may drop. Some children and young adults need to see the practicality of their courses in order to achieve in them, while others do not. If your child is one of the former, you can do something.

One girl had disliked math through her entire school career and was getting a D in that subject in the seventh grade. She had decided that she wanted to be a lawyer—she loved to watch reruns of *Perry Mason,* so her decision was definitely based on this stereotype. She was extremely verbal and did well in English and speech, because she saw the relationship between these courses and her fantasy career. Her parents arranged to have her go to lunch with a woman lawyer, first telling the lawyer about her problem with math. The girl spent two hours with the lawyer and learned what lawyers really did and how math was important in settling divorce cases, accounting problems, and so on. The girl's math grade went up to a B in the next marking period.

This young lady is now sixteen and a junior in high school. She is talking about journalism, public relations, or television and radio as possible career options to satisfy her ideal life-style. She still does not like math but has managed to work through her algebra and geometry classes because she has learned that she needs them to get into college to prepare for these possible careers.

Following is a list of subject areas and careers that use, to some extent, concepts and/or skills taught in these subjects. If your child is one who needs to know the reason for taking and passing certain courses, perhaps you can arrange to have your child talk to one or more people who work in these careers. These lists are obviously not exhaustive and perhaps you can think of others, but they are a start:

109

## English

### A. Careers with an Emphasis on Speaking:

Actor or actress, flight attendant, auctioneer, salesperson, minister, drama coach, drama critic, receptionist, interpreter, lecturer, stage director, personnel worker, politician, public relations worker, radio or TV announcer, speech therapist, teacher.

### B. Careers with an Emphasis on Writing:

Advertising worker, author, technical writer, editor, etymologist, journalist, librarian, medical librarian, printer, proofreader, publisher, reporter, sales correspondent, script writer, stenographer, translator, typesetter, typist, social worker, merchandising worker.

### Mathematics

Accountant, actuary, auditor, financial advisor, statistician, systems analyst, programmer, airplane inspector, airplane mechanic, airplane pilot, auto and diesel mechanic, architect, astronomer, bank worker, broker, cartographer, cashier, chemist, draftsperson, economist, electrician, plumber, construction worker, engineer, engineering technician, dentist, doctor, geologist, home economist, insurance underwriter, investment counselor, machinist, meteorologist, pharmacist, purchasing agent, surveyor, treasurer, appraiser, bookkeeper, exporter, farm hand, insurance clerk, medical technologist, medical records administrator, medical X-ray technologist, merchandising worker, optician, payroll clerk, real estate salesperson, attorney, ticket agent, tool and die maker, dental assistant, dental hygienist, forester, navigator, economist, electronic technician, machine repairperson.

### Foreign Languages

(Although some specific careers recommend having some knowledge of a foreign language, in some geographical areas all careers would choose a bilingual or multilingual person over one who had no other languages, if all other skills were equal. It is an excellent secondary career skill.)
Flight attendant, buyer, civil service worker, customs inspector, foreign service worker, hotel manager, immigration inspector, importer, linguist, interpreter, journalist, missionary, researcher, travel

bureau worker, FBI agent, anthropologist, foreign correspondent, worker in an international agency or industry or organization.

## Science

Agriculture specialist, agronomist, archaeologist, astronomer, cartographer, farmer, geographer, engineer, geologist, horticultural scientist, mineralogist, oceanographer, park ranger, doctor, dentist, anatomist, bacteriologist, laboratory worker, dental hygienist, dental laboratory technician, florist, food and drug inspector, forest ranger, game warden, medical illustrator, photographer, museum worker, nurse, nutritionist, allied health worker (includes over 100 different careers), veterinarian, tree surgeon, engineer, air-conditioning technician, fireman, electronic technician, airline pilot, airline or auto or diesel mechanic, construction worker.

## Social Studies

Attorney, city manager, councilperson, politician, court reporter, foreign service officer, historian, tour guide, librarian, reporter, news correspondent, political scientist, economist, teacher, labor relations specialist, anthropologist, archaeologist, criminologist, curator, genealogist, museum worker, paleontologist, sociologist, writer, minister, social worker, advertising manager, public relations worker, geographer, librarian, researcher.

## Physical Education

Nurse, athlete, lifeguard, athletic instructor, sports store worker, physical therapist, occupational therapist, orthopedic doctor, dentist, golf professional, recreational worker, athletic manager, sportswriter, sportscaster, chiropractor, osteopath, sports illustrator.

There are many others, not only in these subjects but in specialized fields such as art and music. Some of these examples may seem remote to you, but they are listed to illustrate the point that even a remote connection is all that is needed to motivate a young person. You can do this in a family discussion beginning, "How many careers can you name where the worker uses math?"

If your child likes or is particularly good in a subject, this may also be a clue to possible career options.

## How to Involve the Schools

So you think that these ideas make sense but that the schools should be doing something about it too? Perhaps you not only want to help your own children but have discovered from the value games that you are somewhat of an activist. But how can you get the schools moving on the problem?

A national movement called career education has been encouraging schools to initiate programs in these areas. This movement, endorsed by many states and local schools, says, in short, that all teachers from kindergarten to twelfth grade have a responsibility to incorporate career concepts and the career and leisure options of their subject areas into their classroom material. It is a method through which regular subjects normally taught in school can be presented in a different light—that of the world of work.

Career education attempts to make education more relevant to life by bringing the community into the classroom and by taking children out of the classroom into the community. It makes children aware of the many future possibilities open to them, not only in the area of careers but also in leisure activities. The program does not attempt to force children to make early decisions, but provides them with a variety of experiences so that their eventual decisions will be based on reality and not on guesswork. Dr. Kenneth Hoyt, director of the Office of Career Education of the U.S. Office of Education, has led in this effort to motivate school workers to stress the importance of work in all subject areas and at all grade levels.

The first step in involving your children's schools is to find out whether or not your Board of Education has made a stand on this program. If it has, you should go to the superintendent to find out what has been done about it in the district—in other words, to what extent the board policy has been implemented. Boards of education sometimes make policies that are never implemented because no one on the school district's staff has been selected to see that it is done.

If the policy has not really been implemented, be prepared to hear a lot of double-talk and jargon. For example: "Financial constraints have necessitated that this program be prioritized at a lower level than other more critical areas." This means, "We haven't put any money in the program and the reason we made a policy at all was to be considered for federal aid."

112

Or you might hear this: "Rather than implement a program without sufficient research, we have decided to do a needs assessment to determine what type of program the learners in this system need." This means, "We don't know how to get started, so we're fooling around trying to figure out what to do. In the meantime, students are leaving school without any decisions made; but they can always go to college or to community college or take the first job that comes along to put off making a decision." The school can then give impressive data on how many of the graduates go to college—but not on how many finish or how many of those who finish are working in fields related to their college major. This is an embarrassing question for school officials to answer.

If you find that not only does the board of education have a policy but that the school system has actually allocated money and personnel to see that it is implemented, you are lucky. But do not stop there. Go to the school your children are attending and ask what is being done. Principals may not have heard of the director of career education, or whatever the title is. If not, that is the time to exert some parent power.

To begin, remember that you know more than the principal does since you have researched this from the top. Use this to your advantage. You can say absolutely scandalous things, and he or she will believe you. Tell him or her that you want the program "implemented" (a good current educational term) and are going to "monitor" (another in-vogue word) it to see that it is done correctly since it is a board policy and you have had an interview with the superintendent. The principal will learn quickly about the program.

If you are not only interested in the schools where your children attend but in the system as a whole, and if you find weakness in the program even though a policy has been passed, have lunch with the board president and express your concern. Get other parents to call the superintendent and board members also. This tactic will work not only to get an approved policy working but to get one enacted if there is none as yet. Be prepared, however, to be made chairperson of the citizens' advisory committee on career education, a job requiring many long hours of work and including some very frustrating times as well as some rewarding moments.

You as parents can exert pressure for, and in many cases can have significant influence on, school programs. But you must be assertive and thick-skinned; it is not an easy task. Remember, too, when you make your appointment with the superintendent, board member, or principal, that telling them why you want to see them will only give them time to compose a response. If you really want to know what is going on, catch them unprepared.

You may encounter school officials and teachers who are confusing *career education*—which incorporates career awareness, career exploration, decision making, and job-seeking skills—with *vocational education,* a part of career education involving training in specific job skills such as auto mechanics, secretarial work, cosmetology, bricklaying, electronic technology, and woodworking. In other words, vocational education is one component of the broader concept of career education. Knowing this difference yourself will assist you when you exert parent power.

What is the value of vocational education (specific skill training) at the high school level? Mostly it serves to keep disinterested young people in school. Are the students who take these courses actually prepared to move directly into the work force as auto mechanics, cosmetologists, and so forth? Relatively few are. When deciding whether or not your child should take a vocational course, determine first why you and your child are interested in the course. If it is for job entry purposes, find out where the school's graduates are working, then call those establishments to determine their opinion of the graduates of this course. This same procedure should be followed in all high school and post-high school training courses that claim to prepare students for job entry.

Courses in community colleges and private business, trade, and technical schools do not always prepare students for job entry either. It is wise to be suspicious if such schools refuse to give you the following information:

• What companies hire your graduates?
• How aggressive are you in placing graduates?
• What percent of your graduates are now working in jobs related to the training they received here?
• What are the names of some of your recent graduates?

Once you have this information, you and your child can make a competent decision on the value of a vocational course.

## Post-High School Education

Let us assume that you have worked with your children on the activities presented earlier in this book and that they do have—for the time being, at any rate—a fairly good idea of who they are, what skills they have, the kind of life they want to lead, and the career options open to them. But suppose they do not know exactly how to go about getting training or education for job entry?

Many students in this situation use community college or university as a way to put off making a decision for two or four years. But there is ample evidence that college does not necesarily assure employment. In fact, in some jobs it is a disadvantage. If a person with a B.A., for instance, applies for a job that does not require a degree, the employer often assumes that she or he will stay only until finding something better.

The plight of the underemployed is well stated in a U.S. Office of Education monograph by James O'Toole, "The Reserve Army of the Underemployed."[9] Following are some quotations from this publication:

*In a speech, President Ford called national attention to a problem that had been worrying many leaders in business, labor and academia; namely, that the rapid increase in the educational attainment of the work force has been accompanied by a concomitant rise in worker expectations. In particular, the current younger and more highly-educated generation of workers now expects good jobs as their just reward for their many years in the educational system. Moreover, these expectations are compounded by a shift in values among the young. Increasingly, young workers prefer jobs that are interesting, socially meaningful, and offer the opportunity for personal growth over jobs that offer only the traditional and more easily provided rewards of money and security.*

On Work in the post-industrial society:

*There will be continued shifting away from a blue-collar industrial economy towards a white-collar service economy.*
*There will be continued growth in the size of the public and private organizations that hire the bulk of American workers.*
*Government will continue to be the fastest growing sector of the economy.*

*Technology will continue to spread, and machines will replace people on many jobs.*

*There will be a continuing slight reduction in the hours worked per week.*

*To many observers, these trends portend a better world and a higher quality of life. Philosopher Sebastian de Grazia foresees a leisure society in which machines will do the labor and humans will be free for contemplation, creation, and self-development. Manpower specialist Sar Levitan sees greater social and career mobility for workers as many blue-collar workers move into cleaner and higher-status white-collar jobs. Sociologist Daniel Bell looks at the same trends and sees the makings of a more just society, a meritocracy based on knowledge and not on power, birth, or inherited wealth. Economist Theodore Schultz sees a boost in productivity, economic growth, and individual income as education "upgrades" the work force. It is possible to share with these authors their desire for such future occurrences without sharing their sanguine views that these indeed will be the outcomes of present or predicted policies or trends. Another scenario, one far less utopian, can be just as convincingly drawn from the same facts. For example, it appears that the slight increase in free time in the future will accrue to those in the work force least prepared educationally to benefit from true, creative leisure as defined by de Grazia.*

The question, then, is, "What kind of schooling or training should my child have and when should he or she have it?"

If, as parents, you want your child to go to college, perhaps you should assess your own feelings about it by answering these questions:

• Why do I want my child to go to college?
• Why do I want my child to go to a specific college?
• Why do I want my child to go to college right after high school?
• What influences can I identify that make me want my child to go to college?

Have your child answer these questions too, and then share and discuss your answers. If your child has researched career options in this book, she or he will undoubtedly know of the options for training that lead to job entry. Write these down and then use

116

the decision-making model described in the previous chapter to arrive at a plan of action.

It is increasingly evident that students' desire for post high school training must be internalized if they are to perform successfully in that training program. A mother illustrated this principle to me in the following story. Her son, she informed me, was extremely bright (I checked with the school records and he was—parents are sometimes overly subjective in this evaluation). He ranked between the ninetieth and ninety-eighth percentile in all areas, but in his senior year, he announced to his family that he was tired of school and did not plan to go on. He was going to work. The parents did not moralize, nag, bribe, or browbeat him in any way, but simply said, "All right, it's up to you."

The young man worked at a variety of jobs and made good money for his needs: maintaining his car, buying clothes, renting an apartment, and dating. But now, after three years, he has announced that his work does little to stimulate his mind and that the people he works with are not the kind he would prefer as associates for the rest of his life. He wants to go to college, but he wants to do it on his own; so he has begun taking night courses at the local community college, is getting A's and B's, and thinks he would like to be an accountant.

The three years of work and maturity assisted this young man in clarifying his goals. Could some of the activities in this book help him? At age thirty, his needs, interests, values, and life goals may again be different—he may need to repeat the process to determine who he is and what is available in the job world, make a new decision on what he wants, and to come up with a new plan of action.

## The Problem of Being Talented and Gifted

I sometimes feel sorry for children who are talented and gifted. The schooling and education and the careers that people intend for them are often based on very high expectations. And if they do not live up to these expectations, parents, teachers, friends, and relatives all say, "What a waste! She (or he) could do so much better"—or one of a variety of other clichés. Sometimes these gifted children must feel like screaming. Their gifts and talents become a burden to carry through life, for they are almost

117

invariably expected to take the highest level of courses, do better than anyone else, and go into a profession.

There are gifted and talented people working in practically every occupation who are perfectly contented, live satisfying life-styles, and are contributing to society in their own way. Why should we impose our values on what they should do? What right do we have?

There are also many gifted and talented people who have lost their enthusiasm for life for a variety of reasons. I wonder how many would not or could not live up to the expectations others had for them and simply gave up trying? Do your children fall in this category? Please—help them to learn about themselves and to know what they want out of life and how to make decisions, but do not impose your values on them or try to make their decisions for them.

When making a decision about where to go for education or training after high school—and many young people will need training of some sort—be sure to consider more than the costs, career programs, entrance requirements, and so on. Your children should know something of the characteristics of the student body. This often makes the difference between success and failure, whether it is a community college, technical school, or four-year college. The best way to determine this, of course, is to visit the campus before making a decision. This I strongly encourage. Talking to its students is another way to learn about a school community. School experiences can be positive or negative; but, at least to some extent, you can be an influence as to which it could be for your child. Remember, if your child is having a negative experience, use parent power. On the other hand, try to look at the situation objectively and not make a hasty decision. Use the decision-making model: what are your options?

# 7

## CAREER
## THEORIES

You may be interested in the theoretical base for occupational choice. If so, you will find outlined in this chapter the basics of several major theories.

In studying the career choices people have made, I have found few whose choices followed exclusively the pattern of a specific theory. In most cases, though, one can find elements of several theories operating. A person may appear to clearly follow one pattern and then change the base of operation—a fact which leads me to believe that all these theories are merely components of a broader theory. This, however, is only my personal opinion.

All of these theories hold certain elements in common:

• Career choice is a process rather than an event.
• Career development consists of a series of stages.
• The different stages can be identified.
• Different personalities are attracted or repelled by certain occupational environments.
• Needs, both conscious and unconscious, affect career choice.
• Accident plays a large role in career choice and development. (The purpose of this book is to make accident play a less significant role.)
• To some extent, career choice is irreversible. (This means, for example, that a woman who has trained to be a doctor and decides, after five years of practice, that she does not like it may find it difficult—though not impossible—to reverse her decision.)

- The self-concept is influenced by contact with others and changes throughout life.
- Success can have a decided effect on career choice and development.
- A career has an effect on life-style.
- Career decision making consists of many compromises for both the individual and the career.

I accept most of these elements and have made an attempt to incorporate them in the activities and the discussion in this book.

For those of you who like to examine theories, here is a chance to become familiar with a few of them. These descriptions are not in any way thorough, however, and if you are interested in knowing more, I suggest reading one of a number of good books on occupational choice theory. Each theorist has written a book on his or her own theory, of course; but certain other books have made a comparative study of the major theories. One such is *Theories of Career Development* by Sam Osipow.[10]

## Economic Theory

In brief, the economic theory is based on the idea that money is the prime determinant in choosing a career. People who demonstrate this theory choose on the basis of, "Where can I make the most money?" Their career changes are also based primarily on this factor.

## Sociological Theory

The sociological theory states that aspects of society are the prime determinants in the choice of a career, and that these factors can have either a negative or a positive influence. To determine to what extent you and your children are influenced by society, look at the following list and determine which of these factors have had or are having an effect on you and your family. Place a G next to those having great influence, S next to those with some influence, N by those with no influence, and *Neg* beside those with negative influence.

| | | |
|---|---|---|
| family | school | church |
| peer group | ethnic group | neighborhood |
| social class | geographical region | father's job |
| mother's job | | |

economic trends in community or nation
social trends in community or nation

120

Now, choose the factors that have had or are having the greatest influence on you and explain why. Discuss this as a family.

## Super's Theory

Dr. Donald Super, a professor at Harvard University, has done considerable research with young people to determine what, in fact, influences their career choices. He has arrived at the following tenets based on his research:

• People differ in their abilities, interests, and personalities.
• They are each qualified, by virtue of these characteristics, for a number of occupations.
• Each of these occupations requires a characteristic pattern of abilities, interests, and personality traits—with tolerances wide enough, however, to allow both some variety of occupations for each individual and some variety of individuals in each occupation.
• This process may be summed up in a series of life stages characterized as growth, exploration, establishment, maintenance, and decline; and these stages may in turn be subdivided into the fantasy, tentative, and realistic phases of the exploratory stage, and the trial and stable phases of the establishment stage.
• The nature of the career pattern (that is, the occupational level attained and the sequence, frequency, and duration of trial and stable jobs) is determined by the individual's and his or her parents' socioeconomic level, mental ability, and personality characteristics, and by the opportunities presented.
• Development through the life stages can be guided, partly through facilitating the maturation of abilities and interests and partly through reality testing and aid in the development of the self-concept.
• The process of vocational development is essentially that of developing and implementing a self-concept: it is a compromise process, the self-concept being a product of the interaction of inherited aptitudes, neural and endocrine makeup, opportunity to play various roles, and approval of superiors and fellows.
• The process of compromise between individual and social factors—between self-concept and reality—is one of role playing, whether the role is played in fantasy, in the counseling interview, or in life activities such as school classes, clubs, part-time work, and entry jobs.

121

• Work satisfactions and life satisfactions depend upon the extent to which the individual finds adequate outlets for abilities, interests, personality traits, and values; they depend upon establishment in a type of work, a work situation, and a way of life in which the individual can play the kind of role she or he considers congenial and appropriate.

## Ginzberg's Theory

Doctors Eli Ginzberg, Sidney Axelrod, and John Herma have also developed a theory considering career choice as a developmental process evidenced by periods. The first, the fantasy period, occurs from early childhood to about age eleven. The second or tentative period covers ages eleven through approximately seventeen and is made up of the interest stage, ages eleven to thirteen; capacities stage, ages thirteen to fourteen; values stage, ages fifteen to sixteen; and transition stage, age seventeen. In this latter stage the young person is beginning to shift from subjective factors such as interests, capacities, and values to the reality conditions that will play a large part in determining the final choice.

The third period, occurring after age seventeen, is the realistic period. It is made up of three stages: the exploration stage, when the young person is exploring subjects and careers; the crystallization stage, when the young person is able to assess the many factors influencing the career choice; and the specification stage, when the choice is finally made.

## Holland's Theory

Dr. John Holland, a professor at Johns Hopkins University, has developed a theory stating that people fall into certain personality types and that the work world falls into certain occupational environments. It also says that people search for environments that will let them exercise their skills and abilities, express their attitudes and values, and take on agreeable problems and roles. Another tenet of this theory is that a person's behavior is determined by an interaction between personality and the characteristics of the environment.

Following are descriptions of the personality types and occupational environments identified in Holland's theory. Can you and your children determine your personality types? Try it and discuss the results.

## Personality Types

1. The *realistic* type is most sensitive to pragmatic, masculine, and nonsocial influences and least sensitive to social, feminine, and intellectual influences.

2. The *intellectual* type is most sensitive to abstract, theoretical, and analytic influences and least sensitive to materialistic and social influences.

3. The *social* type is most sensitive to social, humanitarian, and religious influences and least sensitive to abstract and analytic influences.

4. The *conventional* type is most sensitive to materialistic and social influences and least sensitive to intellectual and idealistic influences.

5. The *enterprising* type is most sensitive to social, emotional, enthusiastic, and materialistic influences and least sensitive to intellectual, humanitarian, and idealistic influences.

6. The *artistic* type is most sensitive to personal, emotional, and imaginative influences and least sensitive to social, materialistic, and realistic influences.

## Occupational Environments

1. The *motoric* environment—illustrative occupations are laborers, machine operators, aviators, farmers, truck drivers, and carpenters.

2. The *intellectual* environment—illustrative occupations are physicists, anthropologists, chemists, mathematicians, and biologists.

3. The *supportive* environment—illustrative occupations are social workers, teachers, interviewers, vocational counselors, and therapists.

4. The *conforming* environment—illustrative occupations are bank tellers, secretaries, bookkeepers, and file clerks.

5. The *persuasive* environment—illustrative occupations are salespersons, politicians, managers, promoters, and business executives.

6. The *esthetic* environment—illustrative occupations are musicians, artists, poets, sculptors, and writers.

According to the theory, a person gradually evolves a model personality preference leading to educational decisions for specific occupational environments. Eventually he or she will then move within this occupational environment toward a career at a skill level appropriate to his or her abilities and achievements. The quality of this decison is related to self-knowledge and knowledge of the world of work. If either of these is limited, he or she will have difficulty choosing a career. In other words, the better one knows oneself and the occupational environments the better the decision and resulting job satisfaction.

Dr. Holland did some studies to relate parental attitude and development of personality traits and arrived at some interesting results. Fathers of sons in the *realistic* category, he found, valued ambition in their sons and hoped their income would be considerable; fathers of boys in the *intellectual* category valued curiosity; *social* fathers valued self-control; *conventional* fathers wished their sons to be happy and well adjusted; *enterprising* fathers valued happiness, adjustment, and popularity; and *artistic* fathers valued curiosity and independence. Trends for girls were similar, but not as dramatic. These findings did not clearly indicate that parental attitudes are of foremost influence on personality styles. To combine the factors of all the personality theories (the Holland theory, the Myers-Briggs theory in chapter three, and the Roe theory below) would be interesting.

## Roe's Theory

Anne Roe, a clinical psychologist, became involved in career choice theory through her research on the personality traits of artists. She then investigated the developmental backgrounds and personalities of research scientists. From her findings, Roe concluded that major personality differences existed between physical, biological, and social scientists. She also concluded that the personality differences existing between them are to some extent a result of childrearing practices. In short, she proposes that individuals inherit the tendency to react in certain ways. This, coupled with childhood experiences, determines the general styles people develop to satisfy their needs throughout life, styles that have specific and major implications in career behavior.

• The hereditary bases for intelligence, special abilities, interests, aptitudes, and other personality variables usually seem to be nonspecific.
• The pattern of development of special abilities is primarily determined by the directions in which psychic energy is involuntarily expended.

124

• These directions are determined in the first place by patterns of early satisfactions and frustrations.

• The eventual pattern of psychic energies, in terms of direction of attentions, is the major determinant of the field or fields to which one will apply oneself.

• The intensity of these primarily unconscious needs, as well as their organization, is the major determinant of the degree of motivation to accomplish.

• Needs satisfied routinely as they appear do not develop into unconscious motivators.

• High-order needs for which even minimum satisfaction is rarely achieved will be effaced; those of lower order will prevent the appearance of higher order needs and will become dominant and restricting motivators.

• Needs for which satisfaction is delayed but eventually accomplished will become unconscious motivators, depending largely upon the degree of satisfaction felt. This in turn depends on, among other things, the strength of the basic need, the length of time elapsing between arousal and satisfaction, and the value ascribed by the immediate environment to the satisfaction of this need.

On the basis of these statements, Roe has developed eight career groups: science, business contact, organizations, technology, outdoor, general cultural, arts and entertainment, and service. There are also six levels within each group: professional and managerial 1, professional and managerial 2, semiprofessional, skilled, semiskilled, and unskilled.

Research conducted to substantiate Roe's theory is mixed in its findings. There is no doubt that personality does play a part, as implied in chapter three. An interesting question posed by Roe's theory is, do birth order and/or childrearing practices affect one's type as described in the Myers-Briggs theory in chapter three? You were asked to figure out your type by the descriptions given there; do you think that your birth order has affected your personality type? Discuss in your family how this might affect how you perceive the world and how you make decisions.

These are the major theories of occupational choice. In chapter three, one of the activities was a worker interview, beginning with the person's first fantasy career and continuing through his or her entire work history. It might now be interesting for you to go back and attempt to analyze that worker's life and career choices to find out which of the theories, if any, were evident. Following is one such worker history and an attempt to analyze it.

Subject: Mary, thirty-two-year-old woman.

I. Fantasy Occupations:
   A. Airline Stewardess. Reason: Liked to travel.
   B. Bacteriologist. Reason: In love with high school biology teacher.

II. Goals after High School:
   A. College education—essential.
   B. Job.
   C. Marriage.

III. First paying jobs (summer between college years):
   A. Office Clerk at Volkswagen dealership.
      1. Satisfactions:
         a. Enjoyed personal contact with customers.
         b. Liked organizing office files and other general clerical duties.
      2. Dissatisfactions:
         a. Lack of variety in job duties—boring.
         b. Not challenging.
         c. Non—glamorous setting.
   B. Art model at college, part-time.
      1. Satisfactions:
         a. Enjoyed association with art students.
         b. Liked art setting.
      2. Dissatisfactions:
         a. Boring work.
         b. Sedentary work.
         c. Dead-end job—no future.

IV. Additional work experience:
   A. Credit investigator (quality review of insurance applications), 5 months.
      1. Satisfactions:
         a. None—only job available after college graduation.
         b. Paying job.
      2. Dissatisfactions:
         a. Loathed work.
         b. No socializing permitted.
         c. Very confining, regimented work.
         d. Demanded piece-work (volume of production).

126

e. Environment distasteful—one hundred desks with "robots" reviewing applications.
B. Psychiatric aide in hospital psychiatric unit, 1½ years.
　1. Satisfactions:
　　a. All co-workers young college graduates.
　　b. Educational environment.
　　c. Enjoyed taking patients to social events.
　　d. Found clinical conferences stimulating.
　　e. Regular hours (8 a.m.-4 p.m. or 4 p.m.-12 midnight) permitted time for fun-type daylight activities.
　2. Dissatisfactions:
　　a. Weekend work.
　　b. Dead-end job.
C. Social work aide (hospital setting), 6 months.
　1. Satisfactions:
　　a. Assisting master social workers gave impetus to interest in developing same specialization.
　　b. Provided good general background for social work school.
　2. Dissatisfactions:
　　a. Not much to do—time on hands.
　　b. Program not structured, dying.
　　c. Dead-end job.
V. Attended school two years and received master's degree in social work. Also got married.
VI. Additional work:
A. Clinical social worker, 9 months.
　1. Satisfactions:
　　a. Stimulating supervisor who provided supervision yet autonomy.
　　b. Preferred out-patient therapy to in-patient therapy.
　　　1. Liked people on short-term relationship.
　　　2. Liked constant variety of patients.
　2. Dissatisfactions:
　　a. Low salary.
　　b. Felt isolated in in-patient unit.
　　c. Social workers undervalued.
　　d. Unable to be assertive.
　　e. Commuting distance too great.
B. Clinical social worker (different hospital), 5 or 6 months.
　1. Satisfactions

a. Higher salary.
b. Supervisory position over two graduate students.
c. Work varied—individual therapy, family and group therapy.
d. Hours 8 a.m.-4 p.m.
2. Dissatisfactions:
a. Terrible environment—distasteful to senses.
b. Very depressing type of patients.
c. Positive results of treatment gave little personal satisfaction.
d. Unsophisticated staff regarding therapeutic techniques.
C. Community Mental Health Center worker, 3 months.
1. Satisfactions:
a. Beautiful facility.
b. Close to shopping center.
c. Liked working with day treatment center where patients went home at night.
d. Small, close staff—developed friendships.
e. Fun things possible with patients.
f. Responsibility increased.
g. Autonomy existed.

2. Dissatisfactions: Pleasant boss but terrible administrator.

D. Psychiatric Institute worker, 2 years and 2 months.
1. Satisfactions:
a. Substantial salary increase.
b. Training opportunities.
c. Therapy varied, i.e., multifamily therapy, therapeutic family therapy.
d. Loved working with adolescent unit and with families for first time in in-patient unit.
e. Good opportunity to learn behavior modification system.
f. Liked supervisor.
1. Good model.
2. Commanded respect.
3. Supported and defended employees.
4. Encouraged autonomy in employees.
g. Saw program evolve, change, and develop—own ideas implemented.

h. Job description changed from Clinical Social Worker to Primary Therapy Worker, responsible for coordinating treatment.

i. Able to identify with staff, share common problems with other workers—this impossible within multidisciplinary team.

j. Held leadership roles dealing with quality of treatment.
   1. Chairman of Peer Review Committee.
   2. Representative from Social Work Department on Hospital Medical Records Committee.

k. Enjoyed staff in hospital.

l. Supervised two students.

2. Dissatisfactions:

a. On job too long—felt need to go on to something else.

b. Morale of staff low, though on increase.

c. Wanted to specialize, get more training, get another degree.

d. Wanted to get away from emotionally charged atmosphere.

e. Wanted more administrative or teaching work, less therapy.

f. Tired of helping people.

VII. Ten years from now Mary *envisions* following:
   A. Improving self so that job would change along lines of public relations work, administration, or teaching.
   B. Maybe pursue degree in interior decorating and arts and crafts.

VIII. Ten years from now Mary *would like* to:
   A. Remarry and work part-time doing free-lance work in therapy or consultations.
   B. Spend free time in volunteer work and political work, and indulge in love for antiques, crafts, and restoration of old homes.
   C. Fulfill need to express creativity, but at same time maintain at least present amount of income.

IX. Career theories that seem to be operating:
   A. Holland's theory.
   B. Roe's theory.
   C. Ginzberg's theory.
   D. Super's theory.

X. Analysis of history in terms of occupational theories:
   A. Holland's theory:
      Mary is identified as a *social* type. These characteristics ultimately led her to the career choice of social worker. As Holland would put it, she found types like herself and joined them.
      All through Mary's work experience the one job satisfaction that is continually significant is her enjoyment of her work in association with other people, whether patients or co-workers.

   B. Roe's Theory:
      Roe's acceptance of Maslow's hierarchy of needs is borne out in Mary's many jobs as a source of satisfaction of many needs. Mary's first jobs met her physiological and hence her safety needs. She went on to jobs that supplied her need for belonging and for love. Her present job filled her need for importance, respect, self-esteem, and independence as well as supplying her need for information, understanding, and beauty. She is now seeking to fill her greatest need—actualization. Her plans for the future indicate her self-concept, and her eagerness to go on to something else shows her striving for this need. As she put it, she wants now to "indulge herself."
      The social interaction and the social status linked to Mary's jobs were and are the main sources of the satisfaction she derived from her work.
      Mary seems to have met her economic needs and physical needs but not yet her emotional needs. It seems faster to her to meet this emotional need by changing her job than by changing herself.

   C. Ginzberg's theory.
      Ginzberg feels that the process of occupational decision making can be divided into three periods of choices: fantasy, tentative, and realistic. Mary's decisions show that

the process is ongoing, and that these periods of decision making can continue far into one's work history.

D. Super's theory.

Super's system of vocational self-image—one's interests, aptitudes, kinds of skills, and opportunities translated into a vocational setting—is what Mary is now going through. Vocational development is not static, but can be manipulated and influenced by many things. Mary is striving for vocational maturity; she has developed her self-concept and presently does not feel that her job role is compatible with this self-concept. This vocational choice and adjustment process is a testing against reality of her self-concept. As Mary's personal development increases, so will her vocational development increase as she manipulates and modifies her future job role.

# 8

## WORK—
## AN EXPRESSION OF
## GOD'S GIFT

This chapter is written to provide meaning for those who believe to some extent in a Supreme Being who has some influence on one's life, including that part devoted to a career. This discussion is not restricted to any particular religion; it is merely for those who believe in a supernatural intervention.

I have talked to young people who make no career plans, believing that God will direct their lives and that they really have nothing to do with the choice of their career. Many of these young and not-so-young people believe they have been called to serve Him, and therefore are vaguely planning to go into the ministry. Their skills and gifts may not be along these lines, but to them God's call means the ministry. Others separate the belief in God from their work entirely, and so go on to choose careers that, in some cases, are in conflict with their religious values. These people often have a difficult time reconciling their values and end up very dissatisfied with their jobs.

There are those who hold to the puritan work ethic, stating that working diligently is next to godliness and that the more disagreeable the work is the greater the rewards in heaven. There are others who believe that since God will take care of them they need not work at all. They go through life loving everybody and living on welfare or on donations from their parents or other susceptible relatives and friends.

I could spend months researching the holy writings of various religions trying to find portions that would substantiate my own point of view, but I do not plan to do this. Rather, I prefer to appeal to your sense of reason. If, in fact, you are a religious family, I believe that you should incorporate this religion into your life. Your religion should help you to live your life totally and, since a great portion of your life is devoted to work, it should help you in choosing career options that lead to your ideal lifestyle. If God is interested in your life, will he not assist you in this search? If he loves you, will he not expect you to live a satisfying life and have a satisfying career? If, in his wisdom, he created you, would he give you a set of natural gifts, interests, aptitudes, and values and expect you to do something in which you cannot use these natural and enjoyable traits? Unless he is devious, sly, and sadistic (and I do not believe that any scripture poses this image), would he expect you to do work that is not in some way enjoyable to you, meaningful to society, and able to grant you some sense of accomplishment?

It may seem, at this point, that I am contradicting myself, because in an earlier chapter I stressed the importance of leisure activities to compensate for lack of satisfaction in one's job. But I do not believe that all parts of all jobs are enjoyable. People do, therefore, need to gain some of life's satisfactions from other parts of their life. All in all, I believe that God meant all men and women to live a satisfying life. When your life becomes more drudgery than enjoyment, perhaps it is time to reassess values, interests, and skills and to allow God's guidance to open new doors—assisted by a few job-seeking skills on your part. If you can believe this and can help your children to understand it, they and you will understand how this chapter complements the rest of the book.

The book *Adventures In Prayer*, by Catherine Marshall, contains a chapter called, "The Prayer That Helps Your Dreams Come True."[11] In this chapter the author says, in part,

*There are those who are wary of this prayer that helps your dreams come true because they are dubious about praying for material needs ... Rightly, they also ask, "Isn't there danger of trying to use God and spiritual principles for selfish ends? ..." Each is a valid question that needs to be answered. As for whether God means for us to include material needs in our petitions, certainly Christ was interested in men's bodies as well as their souls. He was concerned about their diseases, their physical hun-*

134

ger ... And as for the danger that our dreams may spring from our selfish human will rather than God's will, there are tests for this. Only when a dream has passed such a series of tests—so that we are certain that our heart's desire is also God's dream before we pray—can we pray the Dreaming Prayer with faith and thus with power.

Let's begin by acknowledging that God's laws are in operation in our universe—whether we recognize them or not. We have to cooperate with these laws, not defy them. For example, ask yourself questions like these:

Will my dream fulfill the talents, the temperament, and emotional needs which God has planted in my being? This is not easy. It involves knowing oneself, the real person, as few of us do. [Chapter two in this book attempts to help you with this question.]

Does my dream involve taking anything or any person belonging to someone else? Would its fulfillment hurt any other human being? If so, you can be fairly sure that this particular dream is not God's will for you.

Am I willing to make all my relationships with other people right? If I hold resentments, grudges, bitterness—no matter how justified—these wrong emotions will cut me off from God, the source of creativity. Furthermore, no dream can be achieved in a vacuum of human relationships. Such wrong relationships can cut the channel of power.

Do I want this dream with my whole heart? Dreams are not usually brought to fruition in divided personalities; only the whole heart will be willing to do its part toward implementing the dream.

Am I willing to wait patiently for God's timing?

Am I dreaming big? The bigger the dream and the more persons it will benefit, the more apt it is to stem from the infinite designs of God.

If your heart's desire can pass a series of tests like this, then you are ready for the final necessary step in the Dreaming Prayer! Hand your dream over to God, and then leave it in his keeping. There seem to be periods when the dream is like a seed that must be planted in the dark earth and left there to germinate. This is not a time of passiveness on our part. There are things we can and must do—fertilizing, watering, weeding—hard work and self-discipline.

135

The watering, weeding, hard work, and discipline quoted above are, in my mind, those things mentioned in this book. But although this chapter may only have meaning to those who believe, this book can still provide the self-knowledge and skills to make one's life satisfying.

# 9

---

## PUTTING
## IT
## TOGETHER

---

If your children, to serve their life-style, choose career options based on predictions of the Bureau of Labor Statistics, they may be disappointed by the lack of openings in their chosen career area. These statistics, first of all, are based on the assumption of a recession-free, war-free, stable economy with no changes in the energy picture. In addition, a field with openings today may be glutted in four years as young people, hearing of good opportunities, rush to fill them.

Right now (1977), the field of education is overcrowded. Students have heard this; therefore, fewer than ever are entering this field. According to some predictions, there will be a shortage of teachers again in the 1980s. This, however, is dependent on birth patterns. And as young couples decide not to have children, or young women hesitate to interrupt their careers to have babies, these too may change.

This is why the theme of this book has been to choose a life-style and to plan education to adapt to a variety of jobs, not merely to prepare for a given trade or profession. The most promising fields of today, engineering and accounting, could be overcrowded in a few years. According to the Bureau of Labor Statistics, the typical American changes her or his job *seven* times during her or his lifetime, and her or his career three times.

At the end of the school year 1976, about 1.3 million people received degrees, almost double the number granted degrees in

1966. During this same 10-year period, the number of jobs requiring these degrees grew by only about 500,000. This discrepancy, according to some experts, will become worse by the mid-1980s. After 1985, the college-age segment of the population will decrease and the proportion getting jobs in accordance with their education will increase.

Unemployment among humanities B.A.'s in 1976 was fifteen percent. Jobs in the humanities also pay the lowest salaries—about $825.00 per month in 1977. Other overcrowded fields include law, architecture, and psychology. And only about one-fifth of those granted Ph.D. degrees in the 1970s will find work closely related to their training.

On the other hand, business administration, accounting, economics, engineering, and medicine are particularly good fields right now, as are computer science and computer technology. Other fairly good open fields are hotel and restaurant management, agronomy, horticulture, nursing and pharmacology, technology, and sales. The health field, with its hundred or more allied professions, will also be good for the forseeable future. During the late 1970s white males will be in less demand than women and minorities.

These bits of information are provided to emphasize a point: Help your children to learn what life-style they want, what jobs there are "out there," how to make decisions and seek jobs effectively, and how to be prepared to move into other jobs and careers. The career-aware person is better prepared to recognize an opportunity and to seize it. And in this age of specialization, it is short-sighted and perhaps unwise to plan to stay in one career forever. As a forty-year-old, your child may have difficulty living with an eighteen-year-old's decision.

Have a happy future.

# FOOTNOTES

1. This activity was suggested by "Twenty Things You Love to Do," from Sidney B. Simon, Leland W. Howe, and Howard Kirschenbaum, *Values Clarification: A Handbook of Practical Strategies for Teachers and Students* (New York: Hart Publishing Company, 1972), p. 30.

2. *"Job-O": Judgment of Occupational Behavior—Orientation* (Belmont, Calif.: CFKR Career Materials, 1976), pp. 3–16. Reprinted by permission. A complete specimen set may be ordered for $4.00 at CFKR Career Materials, P.O. Box 4, Belmont, California 94002. The set includes a JOB-O booklet, insert, administration manuals, and JOB-O Job-Title Dictionary. The dictionary includes JOB-O job-title definitions, related jobs, unusual jobs, and charted corresponding characteristics.

3. This activity was suggested by "A Personal Coat of Arms," from Simon, Howe, and Kirschenbaum, p. 278.

4. Stanley R. Ostrom, Self-Appraisal and Assessment Structure: A Guide to Educational and Vocational Planning (San Jose, Calif.: Santa Clara County Schools, 1972), pp. 2–15. Reprinted by permission of the author.

5. This activity was suggested by "What Needs Doing," from John C. Crystal and Richard N. Bolles, *Where Do I Go from Here with My Life?* (New York: The Seabury Press, 1974), p. 88.

6. See Carl G. Jung, *Man and His Symbols* (New York: Dell Publishing Co., 1964).

7. Katharine C. Briggs and Isabel Briggs-Meyers, *Myers-Briggs Type Indicator (Form F)* (Palo Alto, Calif.: Consulting Psychologists Press, 1976) pp. 5–8. Excerpts reprinted by permission of the author. The Myers-Briggs Type Indicator, an instrument for identifying type, can only be given and interpreted by an experienced counselor. If you are interested in having your children take the Indicator test, contact your school counselor, who can obtain the test materials from the publisher, Consulting Psychologists Press, Inc., 577 College Avenue, Palo Alto, California 94306. The newly published shorter form of the Indicator, Form G, is more appropriate for school use than Form F. Complete copies of Briggs-Meyers's booklet *Introduction to Type,* giving descriptions of each of the sixteen types, can be obtained either from the publisher as noted above or from the Center for Applications

of Psychological Type, 1441 N.W. 6th Street, Gainesville, Florida 32601.

8.  See Frances Ilg and Louise Bates Ames, *Is Your Child in the Wrong Grade?* (New York: Harper and Row, 1967).

9.  James O'Toole, *The Reserve Army of the Unemployed* (Washington, D.C.: U.S. Office of Education [Office of Career Education], 1976), pp. 4-6.

10.  Samuel H. Osipow, *Theories of Career Development* (New York: Meredith Corporation, 1968).

11.  Catherine Marshall, *Adventures in Prayer* (Old Tappan, N.J.: Chosen Books [Fleming H. Revell, distributor], 1975), pp. 36-38. Reprinted by permission.

# ABOUT THE AUTHOR

Darryl Laramore received his Ph.D. in secondary school guidance in 1971 at the University of Maryland at College Park. His profession has been highlighted by his desire to help young people choose satisfying careers.

He first became interested in career counseling as a teacher in 1953 in a junior high school in Downey, California, because of his awareness that students who had career goals did better in school than those who did not. Although those goals usually changed, other goals took their places. Those students who had no life goals were less motivated. Laramore began to wonder whether these goals were based on good information or if they were stereotypes that students held of certain careers (i.e., Law enforcement is exciting; flight attendants are glamorous).

In 1967, to his knowledge, he started the first telephone career information center in the country. A career information technician took calls from students and answered questions from current written information. If a student's questions became too detailed, the technician put him or her on "hold," contacted a person working in that field from the hundreds of community volunteers, and put the student and the worker together in a conference call. This operation gained national publicity, and Dr. Laramore was asked to send information about its operation throughout the nation. Some of the more interesting conference calls he remembers were from a roller derby queen, a professional chess player, and several professional athletes. Many students' stereotyped views were exploded during these conferences; others were validated.

From this project he went on in 1971 to develop the first career education program that he knew of in the United States, training six elementary teachers, six junior high teachers, and six senior high teachers to infuse career concepts into their curriculum areas. As a result of this program, he was asked by the California Department of Education to train personnel in the ten original career education sites in California.

In 1973 Dr. Laramore became aware that career information alone is not sufficient but that students and adults must understand and use a process including self-awareness, career awareness, decision making, and job-seeking skills in order to have satisfying lives.

At present he has begun working not only with family groups but with industries to assist their employers in this career-development process. The exercises in this book are used with these groups.

Dr. Laramore also teaches career counseling techniques at Virginia Polytechnical Institute and State College to graduate students in counseling. As he takes these graduate students through the process, many quit counseling and move into other careers, confirming his opinion that adults, as well as children, make decisions based on inadequate information about themselves and the world of work.

He is married and has three children. His wife is a journalism, English, and speech teacher at Paint Branch High School in Montgomery County, Maryland. Nina, nineteen, is a student at Fresno Pacific College working toward a degree in communiations and public relations. Christopher, seventeen, is a high school student interested in business administration and graphics. And Megan, fourteen, is going through the career process now.

Dr. Laramore and his wife are interested in the family and feel that families should work together as a unit. To help parents and children develop their skills, they not only taught parent effectiveness training to parents and children but also wrote a syndicated column at one time entitled "For Parents Only."

In his own life he has applied the career process to help make changes in education. Now he works with industry and families. No one, says Laramore, needs to be trapped in a career if he has the skills to move out of it.

Brigham Young University Press, a member of the
Association of American University Presses, shares fully
the AAUP dedication to excellence in university press
publishing.

At BYU Press we focus mainly—but not solely—on
Western regional studies and early childhood education.

Authors with manuscripts in these and related areas
may submit queries to Managing Editor, BYU Press,
218 UPB, Brigham Young University, Provo, UT 84602,
USA.

143